Bouncing Back

Bouncing Back

SKILLS FOR ADAPTATION TO INJURY, AGING, ILLNESS, AND PAIN

Richard L. Wanlass, PhD

OXFORD
UNIVERSITY PRESS

OXFORD

UNIVERSITY PRESS

Oxford University Press is a department of the University of Oxford. It furthers
the University's objective of excellence in research, scholarship, and education
by publishing worldwide. Oxford is a registered trade mark of Oxford University
Press in the UK and certain other countries.

Published in the United States of America by Oxford University Press
198 Madison Avenue, New York, NY 10016, United States of America.

Library of Congress Cataloging-in-Publication Data
Names: Wanlass, Richard L., author.
Title: Bouncing back : skills for adaptation to injury, aging,
illness, and pain / Richard Wanlass.
Description: New York, NY : Oxford University Press, 2017. |
Includes index. Identifiers: LCCN 2016030399 (print) | LCCN 2016042943 (ebook) |
ISBN 9780190610555 (pbk. : alk. paper) | ISBN 9780190610562 (UPDF) |
ISBN 9780190610579 (EPUB)
Subjects: LCSH: Self-care, Health. | Rehabilitation. |
People with disabilities—Rehabilitation. | Sick—Rehabilitation.
Classification: LCC RA776.95 .W355 2017 (print) | LCC RA776.95 (ebook) |
DDC 615.5—dc23
LC record available at https://lccn.loc.gov/2016030399

This material is not intended to be, and should not be considered, a substitute for medical
or other professional advice. Treatment for the conditions described in this material is highly
dependent on the individual circumstances. And, while this material is designed to offer
accurate information with respect to the subject matter covered and to be current as of the
time it was written, research and knowledge about medical and health issues is constantly
evolving. The publisher and the author make no representations or warranties to readers,
express or implied, as to the accuracy or completeness of this material and do not accept,
and expressly disclaim, any responsibility for any liability, loss or risk that may be claimed
or incurred as a consequence of the use and/or application of any of the contents of this material.

Contents

Preface

It's been my privilege over the past three and a half decades to work with thousands of people as they have dealt with loss of ability from injuries, illnesses, and advancing age. In adapting to such changes, most people need to learn how to restore their mood and self-esteem, manage their stress and anxiety, and deal with the frustration of not being able to do what they could do before. They often need to learn new ways to relate to others whom they are now more reliant on and to form new friendships to replace those that are lost. Many also need to learn how to cope with chronic pain and to develop strategies for dealing with diminished memory and concentration.

Despite their great needs, most of these individuals don't have access to as much skilled therapy as they require and don't find traditional psychological self-help books directly relevant to their loss of ability. To make up for this lack of resources, I developed written self-help materials and revised and updated them over the years based on new research findings and my own and my clients' observations of what actually works for them in real life. With the encouragement of my clients and my colleagues, I then incorporated these materials into this book that addresses the most important challenges in adapting to loss of ability from injury, aging, illness, and pain.

While this is intended primarily as a book for the public, professional therapists and therapists-in-training may also find the content useful for learning additional skills they can teach to their clients. More importantly, this is a book that they can recommend to their clients who are dealing with loss of ability. Physicians, physician extenders, and nurses who are frustrated by the challenge of addressing the adjustment needs of this population may also find this a useful book to recommend.

Because they deserve the recognition (and because expressing gratitude is one of the keys to greater happiness—see Chapter 2), I'd like to sincerely thank the colleagues and family members who provided the most encouragement, creative input, and insightful feedback on this project.

Despite her demanding role as president of the American Psychological Association Rehabilitation Psychology Division, my longtime colleague Dr. Kate Brown took the time to carefully read each chapter and provided many wise and helpful suggestions.

Dr. Ronald Ruff—author of *Effective Psychotherapy for Individuals with Brain Injury*, former president of the National Academy of Neuropsychology, and also a longtime colleague—provided invaluable input and encouragement both in our conversations and in his review of chapter drafts.

Health psychology experts Drs. Daniel Rockers and Amir Ramezani joined me in forming our own psychology writers' workgroup and provided detailed feedback and abundant support.

Dr. Debra Fishman helped greatly both by pilot testing some of these chapters with her chronic disease management groups and by contributing to the design of some of the illustrations used in this book. Dr. Karen Freed also pilot tested these chapters in her groups and provided important feedback and encouragement.

Three medical doctors provided essential support and validation of the accuracy of health-related information. I'm grateful to Dr. Clifford Straehley for sharing his expertise in psychiatry and psychotherapy, to Dr. Peter Gerritz for sharing his expertise in rehabilitation medicine and integrative healthcare, and to my sister Dr. Wendy Wanlass for carefully reviewing every chapter and sharing her expertise in geriatric medicine.

While on the topic of family, I'd also like to thank my sister Dr. Susan Wanlass for reading the entire manuscript with the skilled eyes of an English professor and my sons, Brian and Zachary Wanlass, for ensuring the clarity and suitability of this writing for millennial and military audiences.

Holly Bleasdale, LCSW, and Kevin Wheeler, LCSW, provided helpful feedback from the perspective of social workers with expertise in rehabilitation.

Many current and former rehabilitation psychology and neuro-psychology colleagues from the University of California, Davis, Medical Center also deserve thanks for their helpful suggestions and encouragement, including Drs. Niki Amsden, Michael DeBellis, Lora DeCristoforo, Sarah Farias, Ali Farris, Lindsey Frazier, Kaye Hermanson, Ashley Gunter Hill, Kristin Jacobson, Ronn Johnson, Madeleine Katz, Renee Low, Ekaterina Mahinda, Steven McCormick, Caron Nogen, Louisa Parks, John Thomas, and Robin Timm.

I dedicate this book to my wife, Kelly O'Hagan, and to my parents, Anita and Lawrence Wanlass. Each has provided invaluable support, encouragement, and feedback, and each has personally shown inspiring wisdom and courage in adapting to health- and age-related changes in ability.

I also dedicate this book to the many clients who have allowed me to share in their struggles and successes as they have dealt with major changes in ability. Thank you for trusting in me and for showing me how adaptation works in real life.

Introduction

Whether gradually through the natural process of aging or more abruptly due to injury or illness, we all must deal with changes in physical and mental ability. As humans, we are endowed with many remarkable abilities, each of which follows its own trajectory. Some abilities peak early in life—think, for instance, of the immigrant child who almost effortlessly achieves fluency in the language of her new country while her parents struggle. Other abilities, fortunately, continue to steadily strengthen into older adulthood—think, for instance, of the wisdom and perspective that grow with our decades of experience.

If you're old enough to be reading this, chances are some of your abilities have already declined. Much of this decline is very gradual and easily taken in stride. Even gradual decline in ability, however, eventually reaches a point at which important life functions are affected. At this point, the decline in ability becomes more of a challenge to our coping resources.

Even more challenging are the more abrupt declines or losses of ability that sometimes occur with injury or illness. Examples include traumatic brain injury, chronic pain, spinal cord injury, stroke, amputation, heart disease, cancer, burn injury, diabetes, muscular dystrophy, and amyotrophic lateral sclerosis (ALS)—the entire list is too long to include here.

In over three decades as a rehabilitation psychologist and neuropsychologist, I've witnessed the difficult and often inspiring struggles of many men and women as they've grappled with both gradual and abrupt changes in ability. Their successes, and sometimes their failures, have revealed the coping skills that promote adaptation to change. These skills are reviewed in the chapters that follow.

The reader is reminded that just skimming through these chapters will not be enough to improve adaptation. It will be necessary to put your best effort into changing some of your ways of thinking and behaving. Real change comes through intense focus on specific skills, so you are encouraged to tackle one chapter at a time and to complete all the exercises and worksheets. And because change is difficult, we begin with a review of tools to help you become better at change.

Chapter 1

Self-Management

Changing Behavior and Thoughts

To adapt well to loss of ability, you'll have to make some changes in what you do and how you think. Change, however, is rarely easy. Because ingrained habits and routines resist change, special techniques are needed to break through this resistance. In this chapter, we'll cover some of these self-management techniques.

The first step in self-management is to identify some specific changes you want to make. You may already have some change goals in mind, and as you read the rest of this book, you'll likely come up with additional goals.

Establishing goals is not typically the hard part, though. The real challenge lies in overcoming avoidance and managing your time so that progress toward meeting your goals actually happens.

For example, I had the goal of writing this chapter, but how did I manage my time and overcome my own procrastination? What techniques did I use that could also be helpful to you? Below I'll describe a few scientifically supported methods that really work if you actually use them.

But first, a warning: Just reading about these techniques won't get you anywhere. If you don't actually do something different as a result of reading this chapter, your reading about overcoming procrastination will just be another form of procrastination.

The first rule of time management is: You do not waste time. If you're about to read this chapter but have no serious intention of taking real steps to change your thinking or behavior, please just put this down now because you're wasting your time.

Thousands of hours have undoubtedly been wasted by people reading about time management without actually changing what they do. Don't add to this sad irony. You can always come back when you're more ready to make changes.

You can also come back after you've read some of the other chapters in this book and have more specific ideas about the changes you want to make.

If you're still with me, let's examine some of the other important rules and steps for decreasing avoidance and improving time management so that you can make positive changes in your life.

We'll start by identifying some goals you'd like to pursue but have been putting off or avoiding. We'll also identify the activities you tend to do instead of pursuing your goals.

Use the following worksheet (Table 1.1) to write down a few things you'd like to accomplish and then list what you often find yourself doing instead of working toward your goals.

■ Goals and Avoidance Behavior Worksheet

Table 1.1

A. Goals You've Been Avoiding	B. What You've Been Doing Instead
Example 1: Starting an exercise program	Example 1: Napping
Example 2: Enrolling in a class	Example 2: Browsing the Internet
Example 3: Finding a volunteer job	Example 3: Playing video games
Example 4: Organizing belongings	Example 4: Shopping

Next rank the items in column A in order of priority. See if you can cross out any of the goals toward the bottom of your ranking that are either unrealistic or not very important to you right now.

In column B, rank order the activities in terms of what you enjoy the most or tend to do the most.

As you're about to see, column B is the list of *rewards* you'll use to motivate yourself to accomplish tasks from column A.

That's right, the free ride is over—no more unlimited rewards no matter what you accomplish. If you want to be good at self-control, time management, and procrastination avoidance, you'll occasionally have to apply what psychologists call "Grandma's Rule": *First you work, then you play.*

Not all day every day—sometimes you can just have fun. But if you want to be productive and tackle projects you've been avoiding, you'll have to use self-discipline some of the time.

At this point, you may be saying, "But I don't have any self-discipline; that's my problem." Actually, though, self-discipline is not something you're either born with or not, like having a certain eye color. Instead, it's more like a muscle that everyone has and that can be strengthened over time through exercise.

You may also be thinking, "But I don't want to give up my enjoyment. Life's hard enough." I'm actually on your side here. I don't want you to give up your healthy pleasures; I just encourage you to enjoy them after you've taken little steps toward the goals you were previously avoiding. Once you get the hang of this, you'll probably notice that your rewards are even more enjoyable when they feel earned.

If you actually came up with some items for each list, congratulations— you just demonstrated that you're not a hopeless procrastinator after all. Maybe it's time to start thinking of yourself as someone who gets things done. If you didn't complete the lists, please go back and do so now before proceeding.

Now it's time to select a *goal* from column A that you want to achieve and a *reward* from column B that you'll give yourself when you complete one small step toward your goal.

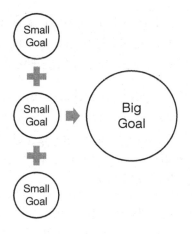

Figure 1.1

Big goals need to be broken down into several smaller goals.

That last sentence introduces an extremely important point: *Your bigger goals need to be broken down into smaller goals*, sometimes much smaller goals (Figure 1.1). As you're starting to become better at self-management, the smaller the goals you choose, the more likely you are to succeed.

For example, I break down the bigger goal of writing a chapter into several smaller goals, such as:

- Jotting down a few ideas about the important points to cover

- Putting these notes into an order that makes sense

- Dictating or typing a very rough draft

- Revising the draft several times

The big goal of writing a chapter seems intimidating enough that I'd probably avoid starting if I didn't break it down into these much easier small goals and reward myself after accomplishing each one of them.

Smaller goals, along with bigger rewards, help you over those humps that almost always stand in the way of behavior change.

What are those humps? One is just *inertia*, or the tendency for things to stay the same. Even really unhappy people tend to find some comfort in routine and resist making changes. You can get over this inertia hump by starting with smaller goals and bigger rewards.

Another hump is *fear*, such as fear of failure or fear that you'll be rejected or found to be not good enough. Part of the solution here is again smaller goals and bigger rewards.

Fear is actually strengthened by avoidance, so the more you procrastinate (avoid), the stronger the fear becomes. But as you break your bigger tasks into more manageable bits and reward yourself for small accomplishments, the fear will lessen because it's no longer being fueled by avoidance.

Smaller goals are also extremely important for addressing another one of the biggest contributors to procrastination: the paralysis caused by *perfectionism*. If your plan is to do a superb, complete job, you may feel overwhelmed, fear failure, and not even try.

If, on the other hand, your plan is just to begin your project in a very rough-draft form, it won't seem so daunting. You can always go back and make improvements later.

Another powerful technique for overcoming fear is to examine and challenge the thoughts and assumptions that activate fear and lead to avoidance. For example, if your goal is to do something creative, such as painting a picture or writing a novel, perhaps you fear criticism and rejection. While almost nobody likes either of these, some people are able to handle them better than others.

What are their secrets? Here are some of the ways they successfully manage fear of criticism and rejection:

- One secret is that they don't set unrealistic expectations. They don't, for example, expect to become the next Michelangelo or Mark Twain.

- They don't catastrophize. In other words, they don't think it will be the "end of the world" if people don't like their work.

- They frequently remind themselves that taste is subjective and that most creative people, even "successful" ones, are criticized or rejected on a regular basis.

- They remind themselves that they're working on their creative project because they enjoy the process of working on it.

- They remind themselves that criticism and rejection may hurt, but they'll get over it and probably be able to learn from it.

■ And importantly, they remind themselves that *self-respect is a choice* they make, not something dependent on outward "success" or on the reactions of others.

■ People who overcome fear and avoidance also have learned to be good at not over-generalizing and not thinking in all-or-none terms. In other words, they don't assume that just because one person doesn't like their work, no one else will. They also don't assume that just because they're not producing work that others like now, they can never do so or that failing at one thing makes them an overall failure.

■ Instead, they remind themselves that talent can be strengthened over time by practice and effort and that failing at one thing doesn't mean that they're failures in general.

■ They take pride in their effort and willingness to pursue new challenges, reminding themselves that any success beyond that is just a bonus.

Do any of these helpful, adaptive thoughts seem familiar to you? How about the unhelpful, maladaptive ones?

If fear is blocking your progress, identify the unhelpful, fear-producing thoughts you're having, challenge them, and develop more accurate and adaptive replacement thoughts.

Then repeat these more adaptive thoughts to yourself on a regular basis, especially when you catch yourself procrastinating.

Habitual ways of thinking are rarely changed overnight, so be prepared to work at this for quite a while. It often takes several months of regular practice for habitual unhelpful thoughts to be "erased" and automatically replaced by helpful ones.

Use the following worksheet (Table 1.2) to write down a few unhelpful or maladaptive thoughts you've been having and some more helpful or adaptive alternative thoughts you'll start having instead.

Table 1.2

A. Maladaptive Thoughts	B. Adaptive Thoughts
Example 1: I know I'm really out of shape, so I'm going to get up first thing in the morning and run a mile.	Example 1: I know I'm really out of shape, so I'm just going to take a five-minute walk before I treat myself to a second cup of coffee tomorrow morning. Then I'll gradually build up from there.
Example 2: I've got to do a great job and impress everyone with the design I promised to create. My reputation is at stake.	Example 2: I'm just going to brainstorm and come up with some rough sketches for the design I promised to create. Then I'll reward myself with a half-hour of TV.
Example 3: I'm feeling nervous about this interview, so I'm going to cancel it and reschedule for later when I'm feeling more confident. I can't take any more rejection.	Example 3: I'm feeling nervous about this interview, but I'm going to go through with it anyway because facing up to challenges makes me stronger. It won't be the end of the world if I don't get selected this time.
Example 4: Failure is terrible and unacceptable. If I fail, I'll feel humiliated, ashamed, and worthless.	Example 4: Failure will sting, but those feelings will pass, and I'll also feel proud that I tried. If I'm not failing occasionally, I'm not challenging myself enough.

To summarize, so far we've covered the important steps of prioritizing goals, breaking big goals into more manageable small goals, and rewarding ourselves upon each successful completion of a small goal. We've also covered ways to handle the fear that sometimes underlies procrastination.

You may be thinking at this point, "That's not enough; my procrastination problem is really big. What else can I do?"

- One extra step you can take is to set up a work environment that has fewer distracting temptations when you're working on a goal. For example, you might shut your phone off or put it in another room. I did much of the writing of this book in an isolated location that kept me free to focus for a few hours at a time.

- You could also structure your environment so you're more likely to remember to work on your goals. If you want to exercise, put your exercise attire or equipment where you'll see it. Use your smartphone or other electronic alarms and put up reminder notes in places where you'll see them.

- Block out specific times to work on your goals and put those times in your appointment book, planner, smartphone, or calendar.

- Make a verbal commitment to someone that you'll accomplish a certain small task by a certain time.

- If the goal is one that can be accomplished with a companion, make a commitment to work on it together at a certain date and time. You're more likely to follow through if you work with a buddy who's committed to the goal. For example, I invited a couple of psychologist friends to join me for "writers' workshop" events in which I worked on this project, they worked on theirs, and we shared encouragement and feedback.

- Also, it's important to make sure the goals you select are really your personal goals, not just goals that you feel like someone is imposing on you. Most of us resent being forced to do things, and we sometimes express this resentment by procrastinating. Think, for instance, of a teenager dragging his feet when a parent tells him to wash the dishes or mow the lawn. We may be well beyond our teenage years, but that doesn't mean we've totally outgrown our desire to assert our independence. So, even if a goal started out as someone else's idea, you might see if you can make it your own. For example, your healthcare providers may have suggested an exercise program, but you can choose to make their goal your own by focusing on the benefits to you of exercising (and the consequences of not exercising). Once you make a personal commitment to a goal, you're more likely to follow through.

- If your rewards don't seem powerful enough, choose new ones. We humans tend to like variety in our rewards, so try to come up with multiple reward options.

- You can also supplement positive incentives with negative consequences. For example, I might still be trying to finish graduate school if I hadn't used the technique of promising friends that I would pay them $50 if I didn't complete a certain amount of work by morning. I stayed up most of the night on a few occasions, but got the job done and kept my much-needed cash.

- Or you might try this even more powerful motivational technique: Write a donation check to an organization that you truly despise, put it in an addressed and stamped envelope, and tell a trusted friend to mail the check if you haven't accomplished your small goal by the next day. I sometimes refer to this as the "nuclear option" because it's very powerful but best reserved as a last resort.

As you begin overcoming procrastination and accomplishing more and more, you'll likely discover that working toward your goals is taking less effort. You may even notice that you no longer need to consciously use all the techniques discussed above. The less you procrastinate and avoid, the less of a barrier fear will be. And the good feelings that come from accomplishment will serve as powerful rewards for your continued productivity. But keep this chapter handy, because it's normal to backslide occasionally, and when this happens, these techniques will help you get back on track.

Chapter 2

Mood Regulation

If you decided to read this chapter, you may have already noticed that loss of important abilities can lead to temporary worsening of mood. Feelings of sadness, grief, and frustration aren't always experienced, but they are common reactions to the type of loss that often occurs with injury, aging, illness, or pain.

The good news is that most people learn to adapt quite well to such change over time. For example, on surveys of life satisfaction, persons with disabilities generally don't differ greatly from those without such challenges, with many reporting full and rewarding lives. Some studies of older people have found them to be happier and less stressed on average than younger people, despite increasing health issues and declining mobility.

The initial process of adaptation to loss of ability, however, can be difficult, and maintaining a positive mood over time often requires extra effort and new coping skills. For this reason, it's a good idea to become more knowledgeable about the factors that influence mood and the specific steps you can take to improve yours.

This chapter presents many techniques for mood improvement. Some will work better for you than others. That's because mood problems have multiple causes. The solutions that work best will be the ones that address the specific causes of your mood problems.

You don't need to master all of these potential solutions. Just find a few that work for you. And don't forget that real change requires real effort; you'll have to put in some time and make improving your mood a priority.

To help organize the many mood improvement methods covered in this chapter, I've broken them down into two broad categories:

- **Behavior**: Mood improvement techniques that work by changing *what you do*

- **Thoughts**: Mood improvement techniques that work by changing *how you think*

First, let's look at how you can improve your mood by changing your behavior.

Increase Enjoyable Activities and Social Interactions

Much of our happiness and satisfaction comes from doing the many activities we enjoy, both solitary activities and social activities. So when a change in physical or mental abilities or a change in circumstances prevents us from doing some of these favorite activities, maintaining happiness and satisfaction can become more of a challenge.

To understand how to meet this challenge, let's look at what's been shown to work. Some of this evidence comes from scientific research, but equally compelling to me are the many successful adaptations to disability I've seen over the years.

Researchers have shown that mood improves when people increase their participation in enjoyable activities. This may seem so obvious that you'll trust my word, but if you're curious to know more, search the Internet for the work of psychologist Dr. Peter Lewinsohn on "pleasant events."

Increasing pleasant events is not, however, always as easy as it sounds when you have less ability to do things than you did before. For example, loss of ability to do your job might leave many hours a week that are now lacking in the enjoyment and satisfaction that came from working and interacting with coworkers. Likewise, if your former recreational activities can no longer be done as before, this leaves a hole in your schedule, a loss of social connections, and a pleasure void.

As just noted, not everyone reacts to loss of abilities and social roles in the same way, and some people seem to bypass a "grieving" or "depression" stage. However, many, if not most, people go through a temporary period of low mood in reaction to such losses. It can be helpful to process grief feelings by talking or writing about the losses and associated emotions, such as sadness and frustration. Shedding tears is common and can be a part of healthy coping.

Grieving is often most intense early on, but can be delayed in some cases, such as with severe traumatic brain injury, when awareness of lost abilities emerges more gradually. It's common for grief feelings to return occasionally, just as they might occasionally return over the years when a loved one has been lost. When abilities decline over time, as with a progressive illness or advancing age, a new round of grieving may occur with each loss of some important function, such as the ability to drive, pay bills, or prepare meals.

While grieving is often important to the process of adapting to loss of ability, other steps are equally important to keep moving forward.

Years ago I was deeply impressed by the wisdom of a young man with a severely disabling injury who said something to this effect:

> Before my injury, there were about 5,000 things I could do, and now they are only about 2,000 things I can do. I could sit around and stay frustrated and sad about the 3,000 things I can't do any more, but I'd rather focus on enjoying some of the 2,000 things I can still do.

Building upon this young man's wisdom, we might look at life as a journey through a vast amusement park, so big that none of us has a chance to try more than a fraction of its attractions in a lifetime.

Some of these rides or exhibits may not interest us. Some may make us sick so we never want to try them again. And some may have lines so long or require so many tickets we decide not to bother. But after eliminating these, there are still thousands of attractions we could enjoy.

Some of these remaining attractions may be off limits to us at various times in life. For example, some might not admit us because we're too tall or too short, or too light or too heavy. And limitations due to injury, age, illness, or pain may further restrict our options.

But even after eliminating those attractions, there are still thousands of interesting things to see and do. There are, in fact, so many options left that we still have more that we could enjoy than we have time on earth to enjoy them. Time is actually the biggest limitation, not loss of abilities. Those of us who maximize our time in the park focus on the rich variety of attractions that are available to us, rather than being bogged down in sadness and frustration over those that are not.

In real life, we're all limited in some ways, but we all have the choice of whether to focus on those limitations or focus on the remaining opportunities. Which do you choose?

In case amusement parks don't appeal to you, this analogy can be adapted to other attractions that do:

- If you love to learn, for example, you might compare the richness of life's opportunities to a university with millions of books, thousands of courses, and hundreds of majors, far more than you'd ever have time to investigate.

- If you have a sweet tooth, you might think of life as being like a sprawling confectionery with whole wings devoted to chocolates, jelly beans, cookies, cakes, donuts, gum drops, pies, and all of your other favorites.

In each of these imaginary examples, there are more options for enjoyment than time to enjoy them. Certain paths to joy and satisfaction may be blocked (e.g., a university department may close or the jelly bean wing may shut down), but many more paths remain.

With creative, flexible thinking, it's often possible to figure out how to *modify old enjoyable activities* so they can still be done, despite some loss of ability. For example, a man who loved hiking to remote fishing spots and wading into rivers learned to enjoy fishing from his wheelchair off a dock. Every year, thousands of people find ways to stay athletically active after a disabling injury or illness, often through the help of organizations such as Disabled Sports USA (http://www.disabledsportsusa.org).

When making such a transition, the initial enjoyment is often less than the enjoyment from doing the sport, hobby, or other activity the old way, but some enjoyment is better than no enjoyment. And with time, new ways of doing old activities often become deeply enjoyable.

The mistake that some people make is to refuse to try modifying old enjoyable activities. While such an initial reaction is understandable, stubborn refusal to try is a barrier to adaptation.

The other creative approach is to *try out potentially enjoyable new activities* that are within your current capability. The reality is that there are more potential sources of enjoyment than any one person has time to explore in a lifetime. So if injury, aging, illness, or pain precludes your ability to do some activities (even with modifications), there are still many other potentially enjoyable activities to try out.

In trying new activities, it's wise to remember that fondness for new experiences often grows over time. So if a new activity you try is only slightly enjoyable the first time, trying it a few more times is probably a good idea to see if your enjoyment grows.

The concept of "acquired taste" is helpful here. After all, who absolutely loves aged cheese, cricket matches, foreign films with subtitles, or opera after just one experience? And yet each of these is beloved by millions of people who've taken the time to acquire that particular taste.

Sometimes it can seem almost impossible to find joy or satisfaction in new activities while still grieving over the loss of old ones. In some ways, it's like the experience people go through when they lose, through death or rejection, a person they love deeply.

In such cases, the brain seems to have become so programmed to derive enjoyment from the old love that anyone new triggers only the tiniest release of pleasure chemicals. The prospect of new love feels almost hopeless. And yet, throughout history, billions of times over, people have proven that they can move on, find new loves, and feel great joy once again.

The same is true for new enjoyable activities; it's ultimately a matter of trying new activities and giving the brain a chance to reprogram itself to find satisfaction and joy in new ways.

One of the problems with depressed mood is that it leaves people feeling like almost nothing they do will be pleasurable or enjoyable. As a result, depressed people tend not to initiate many activities, thinking, "Why bother? I won't enjoy it. Nothing seems fun anymore."

Unfortunately, a vicious cycle develops in which depressed mood leads to loss of motivation, leading to reduced activity, leading to even worse mood (Figure 2.1).

Instead of waiting to feel the urge to do something, the wise strategy is to just go ahead and schedule potentially enjoyable activities and social

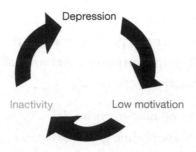

Figure 2.1

Cycle in which depressed mood leads to low motivation, which leads to inactivity, which leads to more depression.

interactions on a regular basis. In my experience, most people who do this find that motivation and enjoyment gradually begin to return.

Before concluding this section, let's focus for a bit on the importance of emphasizing activities and experiences over purchases. It's true that one way to temporarily boost mood is to buy yourself something new, such as clothes, shoes, electronic gear, or jewelry. This mood-improvement practice is so common that it's been given its own nickname: *retail therapy.*

While retail therapy may be good for stimulating the economy, happiness researchers have found that buying things is not as effective as doing things when it comes to getting the most happiness bang for your buck. Planning, doing, and, later on, reminiscing about a vacation, day trip, or even a no-cost outing to a park will generally boost happiness more than making a new purchase.

Including family or friends in your activities can make experiences even more rewarding and memorable. Taking pictures and writing in a journal or on social media can help to prolong pleasurable memories of such experiences.

On the first worksheet that follows, list some activities you enjoyed before your abilities changed and then brainstorm about ways these activities could be modified in order to still gain some enjoyment from them. Then actually schedule some of these modified activities.

On the second worksheet, jot down some ideas of new activities, interests, and social interactions you might be willing and able to explore. Then schedule some of these.

■ **Activity Modification Worksheet**

Write down a few of the activities you used to enjoy before your abilities changed. Then brainstorm about ways these activities could be modified so you can still experience some enjoyment from them.

Activity 1

■ What you used to enjoy doing:

_____

_____

■ How you could modify that activity so you can still enjoy doing it:

_____

_____

Activity 2

■ What you used to enjoy doing:

_____

_____

■ How you could modify that activity so you can still enjoy doing it:

_____

_____

Activity 3

■ What you used to enjoy doing:

_____

_____

■ How you could modify that activity so you can still enjoy doing it:

_____

_____

■ New Activities Worksheet

List some new hobbies or recreational activities you might want to try:

_____

_____

List some new TV shows, movies, or sporting events you might want to start watching:

_____

_____

List some authors whose books you might want to read:

_____

_____

List some friendships you might want to form or strengthen:

_____

_____

List some volunteer work you might want to do:

_____

_____

List some social or cultural events you might wish to attend:

_____

_____

Now list specific steps you'll take in the next few days to try out some of these new or modified activity ideas:

_____

_____

_____

_____

Exercise

Exercise is one of the most effective behavior changes you can make to improve your mood. Research has clearly shown that physical exercise improves mood and self-confidence and, as an added bonus, also helps the brain to function better.

Your old ways of exercising, however, may no longer be possible or safe for you as you age or deal with injury, illness, or pain. Therefore, your healthcare providers should be included in your brainstorming process to determine the best exercise activities for you to do now. Fortunately, exercise doesn't need to be intense to provide mood and health benefits.

Many people start exercise programs only to quickly abandon them. Often they quit because the activity turns out to not be enjoyable enough to keep them motivated. Another common reason for quitting is the soreness or injury that occurs when people don't ease slowly into a new workout routine.

Successful follow-through is more likely if you pick exercise activities you enjoy and if you start very gradually. Having a workout partner also helps.

Exercise doesn't have to be done in a gym. Walking counts, as does gardening or working around the house.

You may be concerned that your already low energy level will be even lower if you start to exercise. Bring such concerns up with your healthcare providers, but in most cases an exercise plan can be developed that actually increases your energy level.

On the following worksheet, jot down some exercise ideas you're willing to discuss with your healthcare providers. Also list some potential exercise partners, places where you can exercise, and equipment or attire you may need to obtain.

Once you have the clearance of your healthcare providers, you might review Chapter 1, Self-Management: Changing Behavior and Thoughts, to remind yourself of strategies that will help you follow through on your exercise plan.

▨ Exercise Planning Worksheet

List some physical exercise activities you think you might enjoy:

_____

_____

_____

_____

Describe your plan for consulting your healthcare providers about which of these exercise ideas would be best for you:

_____

_____

_____

List some people you might want as exercise partners:

_____

_____

List any equipment, attire, gym memberships, or transportation assistance you'll need to start your exercise plan:

_____

_____

_____

State your specific plans for what you'll do to begin exercising, including when, where, and with whom:

_____

_____

_____

_____

_____

In addition to consulting your healthcare providers about an exercise program, talk to them about your mood to see if there's any way they can help to improve it.

Sometimes low mood is a result of correctable medical problems—for example, low thyroid levels that could be detected with a lab test. Have you had a thorough medical exam recently to check for problems of this type?

Depressed mood is also sometimes a medication side effect. For each of the medications you take, look on the Internet at a reputable site, such as http://www.drugs.com, to see if depression is listed as a possible side effect. If you don't have Internet access or are not familiar with how to do this kind of research, just ask your pharmacist about your medications' common side effects. Don't actually change your dosages or stop taking your medications without first consulting with your healthcare providers.

Mood can also be affected by nutrition, so talk to your healthcare providers about your diet. Ask whether they recommend any changes, such as more fish oil or less sugar or alcohol.

Other health behaviors, such as obtaining adequate sleep, can also affect mood, so discuss these as well. Additional information about improving sleep can be found in Chapter 7, Pain Management.

If low mood persists and interferes with your ability to function, talk to your healthcare providers about a referral to a psychotherapist, a trial of antidepressant medication, or both. If tempted to just try the medication approach, keep in mind that outcome research generally supports the combination of psychotherapy and medication as being most effective. Pills alone are often not sufficient to change counterproductive thoughts, beliefs, and behavior patterns.

If your health insurance allows you multiple options for psychotherapists, try to find one with experience in helping people adapt to changes in ability like the ones you're experiencing, perhaps by calling a local rehabilitation hospital or unit for recommendations. *Rehabilitation psychologists* are specially trained for this type of treatment. However, effective psychotherapy can also be provided by clinical psychologists, neuropsychologists, social workers, psychiatrists, and other licensed mental health therapists.

Feel free to call and talk to a psychotherapist for a few minutes by phone before making an appointment. This will help to give you an idea about the person's background, including experience in dealing with problems similar to yours, and interpersonal style. You obviously want someone you'll be comfortable talking to, and therapy works best when you like and trust your psychotherapist and feel that he or she genuinely cares about your well-being. If your first psychotherapist doesn't work out, see if you can find one who's a better match.

As with psychotherapists, not all antidepressant medications are equally effective for everyone. You may have to try two or three until you find one that works well for you. When trying an antidepressant, patience is required because these medications don't work instantly. In fact, they usually take a few weeks to start working. So don't switch before giving each one a fair trial.

Also, remember that antidepressant medications need to be taken as prescribed every day. You can't just take them on an as-needed basis when you're having an especially bad day or skip them on extra good days.

Like all medications, antidepressants can have unwanted side effects. If you experience any problems you think might be related to side effects, let your prescribing healthcare provider know so that any needed medication adjustments can be made. Some side effects diminish over time, but some don't.

Most antidepressant medication prescriptions are written by primary care providers, and that usually works out fine. But keep in mind that the most expertly trained prescribers are psychiatrists (and specially trained psychologists in some areas). In certain situations, it's a good idea to ask for a referral to such a specialist. Examples of such situations include the following:

- A history of high and low mood swings or previous diagnosis of bipolar disorder

- Other complex personal or family psychiatric history

- The presence of suicidal thoughts or self-destructive acts

- Failure to respond to previous antidepressant medication trials

If your lowest moods tend to occur during months with less sunlight, talk to your healthcare providers about whether you might have seasonal affective disorder (SAD) and whether light therapy might help.

Use the following worksheet to help you investigate possible health-, nutrition-, or medication-related contributors to low mood and plan how you'll talk to your healthcare providers about these.

▣ Mood, Health, Nutrition, and Medication Worksheet

Describe your last medical check-up.

How recent and how thorough was it?

_____

_____

Did you have lab tests performed, and if so, was anything out of the normal range?

_____

_____

How thoroughly did you discuss your nutrition and alcohol or drug use?

_____

_____

How thoroughly did you discuss your amount and quality of sleep and your sleep habits?

_____

_____

How thoroughly did you discuss your mood and whether you might benefit from treatment for depression?

_____

_____

Now write the specific mood-related questions you still have and state what your plans are for getting answers to these questions from your healthcare providers or from other sources:

_____

_____

_____

_____

_____

_____

Perform Acts of Kindness

Another effective way to improve mood is to do nice things for others. In fact, researchers on the science of happiness consistently find kindness, or altruism, to be a powerful contributor to well-being.

Altruism, as commonly defined, involves showing kindness to others without expecting anything in return. In reality, though, most of us are "hard-wired" to feel good when we're kind to others, so it actually makes sense to expect some mood improvement as a reward for our good deeds.

If you're struggling to adapt to your own limitations, you may feel like you don't have the energy or resources to help others. But kindness doesn't have to involve large sums of money, lots of time and energy, or great self-sacrifice. Small acts of kindness can be as powerful as large ones. Something as simple as a smile or friendly greeting can improve a stranger's mood and thereby improve your own.

Physical limitations may prevent you from building houses for Habitat for Humanity, but you can probably be a patient and interested listener to a lonely person who wants to talk. You probably also know some people who are going through difficult times and could use a little support. You may even find some people going through the same kinds of adjustments you're going through who'd appreciate your taking the initiative to connect with them.

The Internet opens up additional possibilities for altruism from the comfort of your home. For example, you might find online support groups that allow you to be helpful to others.

Or you might find worthy causes you can support through online petitions promoted by organizations such as http://www.change.org. Through joining forces with others in this way, you can achieve some powerful results in support of causes that are meaningful to you.

If you run out of family members, friends, and strangers to be helpful toward, don't forget that you can improve your mood through kindness and nurturance to animals and even to plants. Caring for pets and gardening have both been shown to improve mood.

On the following worksheet, jot down a few ideas of ways you can show kindness to others. Then, as an experiment, try some of these out, observing what actually does make others, and you, feel a little happier.

▩ Acts of Kindness Planning Worksheet

List some ways you can show kindness to your family members:

_____

_____

List some ways you can show kindness to your friends:

_____

_____

List some ways you can show kindness to others going through adjustments similar to yours:

_____

_____

List some ways you can show kindness to strangers:

_____

_____

List some ways you can show kindness to animals or plants:

_____

_____

Describe some specific plans for acts of kindness you'll perform over the next few days:

_____

_____

_____

_____

_____

_____

_____

Change Your Environment

Sometimes something as simple as a change in environment can improve mood. Such change can be accomplished by moving to a different location, even just going outside or into another room.

Often a change in location will disrupt a negative train of thought and improve mood. Going to visit a friend or relative can have this effect, as can being out in nature or in a public setting, such as a coffee shop.

Another way to improve mood by changing your environment is to modify the places where you spend the most time. Researchers have shown, for example, that mood is enhanced, both short and long term, by simply putting indoor plants where they can be regularly seen. Other mood-improving environmental changes might include opening curtains to let in more natural light, cleaning away clutter, or displaying photos of past vacations, friends, and family.

As mentioned earlier, some people's moods are very sensitive to the amount of exposure they have to bright, natural light. In months with less sunlight, especially in regions far from the equator, insufficient light exposure can cause episodes of depressed mood. This condition is called *seasonal affective disorder* (*SAD*).

If injury, illness, or some other condition causes these light-sensitive people to spend less time outdoors, SAD episodes can occur even during the sunny time of the year.

If you think your mood is sensitive to the season of the year or the amount of sunlight exposure you receive, talk to your healthcare providers about your options, including spending more time outdoors.

Getting out in the bright morning light is generally best because the risk of skin damage from the sun is less than at midday. Also, the bright morning light helps to set the brain's internal clock, often making it easier to sleep well at night.

If your physical condition makes it difficult to get outside or there isn't much sunlight available, talk to your healthcare providers about special light boxes that can be purchased for use indoors to make up for the lack of sunlight. Sitting by these light boxes for a while each day measurably improves well-being in many people with light-sensitive mood or SAD.

■ Environment Change Worksheet

Next time you're feeling in an especially low mood, rate how depressed you feel on a 0–100 scale, with 100 representing the worst depression you can imagine. Then go outside or switch to another location and rate your mood again after about 15–30 minutes. Then come back here and write about what effect changing locations had on your mood:

_____

_____

_____

_____

List some simple changes you could make in your living or working environment that might improve your mood, such as putting indoor plants where they can be regularly seen, opening curtains to let in more natural light, clearing away clutter, or displaying photos of past vacations, friends, and family:

_____

_____

_____

Pick at least one of those changes you listed above and try it out for a few days. Then come back here and describe what you noticed:

_____

_____

_____

Describe what is meant by SAD and state whether you think this condition is one that you should discuss with your healthcare providers:

_____

_____

_____

_____

_____

Smile and Laugh

Smiling and laughing are not the behaviors most of us think of when our mood is low. The natural tendency is to assume that smiling and laughing will just have to wait until something else happens to improve our mood. The reality, though, is that there's a two-way street between how we feel and how we act. Yes, feeling low in mood makes us less likely to smile and laugh. But the opposite is also true: Smiling and laughing improve mood, even when we did not feel happy or find anything amusing before we smiled and laughed.

We don't have to smile at anyone; just activating our smile muscles improves mood. For example, researchers have shown that merely holding a pencil in the mouth in a way that simulates smiling improves mood. While smiling in private works to improve mood, smiling around others can have extra benefits. Smiling in a friendly way around others tends to bring out positive reactions from them, which adds further to the mood improvement.

The same is true for laughing: Deliberately laughing improves mood, even when alone and when nothing funny is going on. And laughing with (not at) others brings the extra benefit of strengthening social connections, which are very important to mood.

For an amusing demonstration of the power of laughing, try searching the Internet for videos of "laughing meditation" groups. If you can find such a group where you live, great, but regularly watching or listening to comedy shows, or just hanging out with funny people, can also improve your mood and general outlook.

In addition to improving mood and strengthening social ties, laughter also has positive effects on physical health, for example, by boosting the immune system, lowering stress hormone levels, and decreasing pain.

So even if you don't yet feel very happy and don't have an urge to smile and laugh, do it anyway. You'll likely improve your mood a bit. Do it enough, and eventually you'll probably get to the point where smiling and laughing flow more naturally. Don't wait until you're happy; smile and laugh first, and you'll invite the happy feelings to come.

On the following worksheet, write some plans for increasing your smiling and laughing.

Smiling and Laughing Worksheet

List some of the benefits of smiling and laughing:

_____

_____

_____

_____

List your plans for using reminder notes or other methods to prompt yourself to deliberately smile and laugh more over the next few weeks:

_____

_____

_____

_____

List your plans for enjoying funny TV shows or other humorous entertainment over the next few weeks:

_____

_____

_____

_____

List some names of cheerful or funny people you know and your plans for spending more time with them over the next few weeks:

_____

_____

_____

_____

_____

_____

Aside from doing more enjoyable activities and changing some of the other behaviors we've just worked on, what else can be done to increase happiness? A lot of our happiness depends on what and how we think. Two people can be in the same difficult situation, and yet one might be happy and the other miserable just based on what and how they're thinking.

The causal link between thoughts and feelings has been recognized for centuries in philosophy and literature. In the last several decades, stimulated by the pioneering work of psychologist Dr. Albert Ellis, this causal link has been developed into powerful psychotherapy techniques for mood improvement.

The basic premise of these techniques, now commonly referred to as *cognitive psychotherapy*, is that certain thoughts and styles of thinking lead to unhappy mood, which can be corrected by changing thinking.

One of these unhealthy types of thinking is excessive self-criticism. In the next section, we'll examine how self-critical thinking following a change in ability can lead to depressed mood, and how to correct this way of thinking to improve mood.

Practice Self-Acceptance

Researchers have found that self-acceptance is one of the keys to overall satisfaction with life. People who are kind to themselves and think they are okay as they are tend to be happier than people who are critical of themselves.

Unfortunately, following a decline in or loss of ability, it's easy to slip into the trap of self-critical thinking. This is especially an issue when the loss involves the ability to do something that was very important to us, such as a career or a favorite sport. While it's okay to grieve over such losses, it's generally unhealthy and unhelpful to be self-critical about them.

Self-criticism is another vicious cycle to watch out for and try to reverse: Self-critical thinking leads to depressed mood, and depressed mood leads to more self-critical thinking.

Take a few minutes and see if you can recall any recent self-critical thoughts you've been having. Perhaps some of these common examples will ring a bell for you:

■ "I'm a failure."

■ "I'm not the provider for my family that I should be."

■ "I'm not a real (man/woman) anymore."

■ "I'm unattractive."

■ "I'm worthless."

■ "I'm just not what I once was."

Each of these self-critical thoughts can be transformed into a more positive thought that helps to improve mood. Here are some examples:

■ "I'll consider myself a success as long as I keep doing the best I can."

■ "I'm contributing to my family the best I can right now."

■ "I can show my strength in ways that don't involve muscles."

■ "I can still be attractive as a person without having to be physically beautiful."

■ "I'm finding new ways to contribute and be of value to my family and friends."

■ "I'm going to take this opportunity to become a better person overall, even if there are some things I can no longer do."

How can you come up with these kinder, less judgmental, and more accepting thoughts to replace the self-critical ones? It often helps to think of how you'd respond if family members or close friends made such self-critical statements. Would you support their self-criticism or would you encourage more self-acceptance? Like many people, you may be much harder on yourself than you are on those you love.

On the following worksheet, you'll be asked to write down some of the self-critical thoughts you've been having. Then you'll be asked to write kinder, less judgmental, and more accepting thoughts you can use to replace the self-critical ones that are worsening your mood.

Once you've come up with the more positive, alternative thoughts, practice saying these kinder thoughts both in your head and out loud. Practice enough that you really learn them.

Then begin the habit of saying these more accepting thoughts to yourself several times each day. Try to catch yourself as soon as self-critical thoughts occur and replace these self-critical thoughts with the more accepting ones you've generated.

Over the course of hundreds of repetitions of this, you can gradually shift your thinking and thereby improve your mood and sense of self-worth.

■ **Self-Acceptance Worksheet**

Write down a few self-critical thoughts you sometimes have:

_____

_____

_____

_____

_____

Write some kinder, less judgmental, and more self-accepting thoughts you could have instead:

_____

_____

_____

_____

_____

Write down your plans for reminding yourself to be on the lookout for self-critical thoughts (e.g., putting up reminder notices or asking someone to point them out to you):

_____

_____

_____

_____

_____

Write down your plans for where and when you'll practice thinking and saying these new kinder, less judgmental, and more self-accepting thoughts:

_____

_____

_____

_____

_____

Focus on the Positive

When mood is low, the mind tends to pay attention to negative things. Unhappy, hurtful, and regrettable experiences from the past are more easily recalled, while positive past experiences seem distant and unimportant. Failures are magnified and seen as proof of our inadequacy, while successes are minimized and attributed to luck or someone else's efforts. Negative aspects of current experiences become the center of focus, as positive events are ignored or discounted. Thoughts about the future tend to focus on negative outcomes, with hope replaced by despair.

This tendency to focus on the negative becomes another vicious cycle in which low mood leads to negative thinking, which further lowers mood, and so on.

The way out of this depressive vicious cycle is conscious, deliberate focus on more of the positive when recalling the past, experiencing the present, and anticipating the future.

This doesn't mean total denial of problems from the past, present, or future. Painful lessons of the past can still be recalled as a way to avoid making similar mistakes. Problems in the present must be perceived and acknowledged in order for corrective steps to be taken. And the possibility of undesirable outcomes must be recognized in planning for the future. What needs to be changed, though, is the balance of positive and negative.

Past: Regarding the past, painful but valuable lessons can still be acknowledged while also cultivating an attitude of understanding and forgiveness toward yourself and others. It's not necessary to like or approve of what you or others did in the past. You can learn what not to do in the future while letting go of guilt and grudges. If you can begin to see past errors, yours and others', as the results of imperfect people doing their best at the time with limited knowledge and skills, you're on the right track.

The next step is to turn your attention toward what was valuable, admirable, or enjoyable from the past and spend more time focusing on this than on regret or resentment.

To help in this process, complete the writing exercises on the following worksheets.

■ Positive Focus Worksheet: Own Past Actions

Write a few lines about something you did in the past that's still upsetting to think about:

_____

_____

_____

_____

Write some negative self-evaluations you've made about this past behavior:

_____

_____

_____

_____

Think for a few minutes about any valuable lesson or lessons you may have learned from this past experience. Write a few lines about what you've learned:

_____

_____

_____

_____

Write some examples of forgiving, understanding, and compassionate statements you can make to yourself from now on about this past event:

_____

_____

_____

_____

_____

_____

_____

_____

Positive Focus Worksheet: Others' Past Actions

Write a few lines about something others did in the past that still upsets you to think about:

_____

_____

_____

_____

_____

Write some negative thoughts you still have about this past event:

_____

_____

_____

_____

Think for a few minutes about any valuable lesson or lessons you may have learned from this past experience. Write a few lines about what you've learned:

_____

_____

_____

_____

_____

Write some examples of forgiving, understanding, and compassionate statements you can make to yourself from now on about this past event:

_____

_____

_____

_____

_____

Present: Excessive focus on negative aspects of the present also needs to be addressed.

If there are specific, fixable problems in your current situation, then focus on the problems only long enough to develop and implement solutions to them. Otherwise your mood will benefit from your conscious decision not to dwell on what you don't like and to *focus instead on what you like.*

Complete the first of the following two worksheets to help you recognize areas of current excessively negative focus, as well as the more positive aspects of your situation that you're willing to focus on more.

Future: Excessive *pessimism* about the future also needs to be challenged and countered with more *optimism.*

Yes, it's true that many undesired outcomes will occur during the course of life, but many desired outcomes will also occur. And you're more likely to *notice and appreciate* these positive outcomes if you're optimistically on the lookout for them.

Even when an undesired outcome occurs, there's often a "silver lining" to that undesired outcome. Sometimes the silver lining will be obvious, but often you'll have to look a little deeper to find it.

Researchers have found that optimistic people are generally happier and more successful in life. Pessimism breeds hopelessness, which leads to inaction. This inaction prevents the positive changes that could bring greater satisfaction.

To help you learn how to counter excessive pessimism with greater optimism, complete the second of the following two worksheets.

▨ Positive Focus Worksheet: Present Situation

List a current problem in your life that you can realistically correct:

_____

_____

_____

_____

_____

List steps you'll take to address this correctable problem:

_____

_____

_____

_____

_____

List some negative aspects of your current situation that you're unproductively focusing on:

_____

_____

_____

_____

_____

List some positive aspects of your current situation (including people, activities, and environment) that you'll consciously choose to focus on instead:

_____

_____

_____

_____

_____

■ Positive Focus Worksheet: The Future

Think for a few minutes about some pessimistic thoughts about the future that you've been having and write them down here:

_____

_____

_____

_____

For each of these situations you came up with, try to think of some potential positive outcomes that you could choose to focus on instead and write them down here:

_____

_____

_____

_____

Now think about some active steps you can begin taking to increase the likelihood of positive outcomes actually happening and write them down here:

_____

_____

_____

_____

_____

_____

_____

_____

Another powerful way to improve mood is to focus on what we still have to be grateful for, despite any loss of ability.

As noted earlier, it can be helpful to acknowledge losses, express feelings about them, and then move on. When we move on, an adaptive direction to go is toward *gratitude*.

Thankfulness can be felt and expressed for good fortune we've experienced in both the past and the present. Despite loss of ability, what can we still find in our past or present to feel grateful about?

Even though loss of ability can pose great challenges, is there any way we can find a "silver lining" or hidden blessing in the changes that have occurred? Many people who've experienced a life-changing disability have spoken about how they've risen above this loss to become in some ways a better person, often a kinder, more compassionate, less judgmental person.

Researchers, such as psychologist Dr. Robert Emmons at the University of California, Davis, have shown that focusing on gratitude can have surprising benefits. Most of his studies involve subjects writing a few sentences a day, or even just a few sentences a week, about things they're grateful for and appreciate. This focus on gratitude and appreciation quite consistently leads participants to feel better about their lives and less stressed and anxious compared to research subjects who write about other topics. Health benefits of practicing gratitude include better sleep, stronger immune system, and fewer visits to physicians.

Another psychological researcher, Dr. Martin Seligman, has shown that writing and personally delivering a letter of gratitude to someone resulted in a large increase in self-rated happiness that lasted for a month.

On the following worksheet, list some things for which you feel gratitude. Then think of ways you can incorporate grateful thoughts and acts into your life. Perhaps you can write thank-you notes or thank people in person more often. And perhaps you can make a regular habit of thinking, talking, and/or writing about those things for which you feel grateful.

If you pray, you might try incorporating more gratitude into your prayers. If you meditate, you might try focusing your meditation on what you're appreciating.

Free gratitude journal apps are available for smartphone users, as are gratitude websites (e.g., http://www.thnx4.org) for computer users.

Gratitude Worksheet

On the lines below, list some things for which you feel gratitude:

_____

_____

_____

_____

_____

_____

_____

_____

Now write down your plans for specific ways to incorporate more regular experience of gratitude into your daily life:

_____

_____

_____

_____

_____

_____

_____

_____

_____

A major change in ability can throw a monkey wrench into our sense of who we are, what we take pride in, and what we see as our purpose in life. That type of disruption can be devastating, often contributing to depressed mood and loss of sense of purpose, identity, and self-esteem.

It's not easy, for example, to go from being

- a successful _____ (fill in professional identity here) to being retired or disabled,

- a skilled _____ (fill in athletic or other talent status here) to being someone who can no longer perform at that level, or

- a person who took pride in his or her _____ (fill in physical attribute here) to being someone who no longer stands out in that way.

Eventually though, most people reach a new equilibrium. And they do this by rethinking who they are and what their purpose in life is.

This important process has been well described by my colleague, rehabilitation neuropsychologist Dr. Ronald Ruff, in his excellent book, *Effective Psychotherapy for Individuals with Brain Injury.*

Dr. Ruff shares the story of a young man who was devastated by injury and loss of ability that left him feeling that his future was "meaningless." In conversation with Dr. Ruff, though, this young man came to realize whom he looked up to most (a grandparent) and what *values* that person represented (love, dependability, and toughness but fairness). He was able to see that these were core values that he could still live by, despite his brain injury, and he went on to re-engage with life around him and feel that his own life was once again meaningful.

Over the years, I've had the good fortune of knowing many people who have gone through a similar process. Clarifying values leads to a stronger sense of purpose, and acting on those values builds a stronger sense of identity and self-worth. Often these people have come to see themselves as more loving and devoted to their families. Many have described becoming more compassionate toward others, less judgmental, or more spiritual. Some have committed themselves to a cause, such as protection of the environment, animal welfare, or disability rights.

For example, a former corporate executive with a recent spinal cord injury decided to find new meaning and purpose in his life by helping others with disabilities. Despite losing use of his legs and having only limited use of his hands and arms, he retained the persuasiveness, organization, and leadership that made him a success in business. He used these skills to build a social organization for persons with disabilities, persuading local businesses to sponsor their activities. He also trained to become a peer counselor so he could more effectively mentor others dealing with loss of ability, and he became active politically as an advocate for the rights of persons with disabilities and of their caregivers.

In another example, a 24-year-old athlete had her Olympic aspirations derailed by a spinal cord injury. She chose to stay true to her love of sports, but shifted her focus from competing to teaching and being a fan. As an elementary school physical education teacher for three decades, she has nurtured an appreciation for sports and sportsmanship in hundreds of children (including mine), staying in touch with many over the years and supporting as a fan those who have gone on to compete at higher levels. In her time off from teaching, she has traveled the nation and the globe, attending the Olympics, World Cup, Super Bowl, and World Series and other major sports and entertainment events too numerous to recount here. When she was honored as an Olympic torch bearer, her current and former students, and their grateful parents, lined the streets to cheer her on.

To help you think about your own identity and purpose, please use the following worksheet to write a few lines about how you identified yourself, what you took pride in, and what your sense of purpose was before you experienced a decline in ability that caused these things to change.

Then take some time to think about your most important values. It may be helpful to think of those personal contacts and historical or fictional characters you've admired most. What qualities do they exemplify? Then think about those qualities within yourself that you value and still retain despite any loss of ability.

Write a few lines about how you identified yourself, what you took the most pride in, and what you saw as your purpose in life before your abilities changed:

_____

_____

_____

_____

Think about those people you've looked up to most in your life, for example, family, friends, teachers, coaches, mentors, bosses, or even historical figures or fictional characters. What values or characteristics of theirs do you most admire?

_____

_____

_____

_____

Think about how you'd like to be remembered at the end of your life. Write down what you'd want to have said about you and the way you lived:

_____

_____

_____

_____

Based on what you wrote above, list the values that are most important to you and write down some ways you can chose to act on those values:

_____

_____

_____

_____

_____

Over the next few weeks and months, continue to think about what your important values are and how you can act on them in ways that make you feel good about who you are and what your purpose in life is. Think about how your strongest values translate into specific actions you can still take, and then begin taking those actions more and more. In doing so, you'll gradually reshape your identity and sense of purpose in ways that improve your mood and self-worth.

Conclusions

The goal of this chapter is not for you to achieve complete happiness and satisfaction. That's unrealistic. Life is difficult. Sadness is part of the normal range of human emotions. Episodes of unhappiness, frustration, guilt, anger, and various other unpleasant emotions will still occur, and there's no need to feel like a failure when they do. Just recognize that, when they do, they're only temporary states that will eventually pass, and that you can hasten their departure by using the mood management techniques you've learned.

If you're interested in additional reading about ways to improve your mood, a valuable resource is *Feeling Good: The New Mood Therapy*, by psychiatrist Dr. David Burns. While it's not specifically focused on mood improvement following loss of ability, this book's effectiveness for general mood improvement has been established by independent researchers. More information on this outcome research can be found on Dr. Burns' website: http://www.feelinggood.com. For an entertaining and informative presentation by Dr. Burns, search with your Internet browser for his TED Talk entitled "Feeling Good."

Chapter 3   *Stress and Anxiety Management*

Almost everybody experiences some stress and associated anxiety and tension on a regular basis. While not particularly comfortable, these reactions can be valuable in alerting us to pay extra attention when we perform important tasks or find ourselves in high-risk situations.

Sometimes, however, the stress response is triggered too easily or too intensely, causing unnecessary discomfort. In these cases, it helps to learn techniques to regulate the stress response.

Stress management skills are especially useful when dealing with major life challenges, such as those that occur when abilities change as a result of injury, aging, illness, or pain. A recent survey by the American Psychological Association found that American adults who have a disability are almost twice as likely as those without a disability to report an "extreme" stress level (defined as a score of 8, 9, or 10 on a 10-point scale). More information about this survey and additional stress management resources are available on the Internet at: http://www.apa.org/news/press/releases/stress/index.aspx.

Understanding Stress and Anxiety

What Are Stress and Anxiety?

Stress occurs when the demands we place on ourselves or others place on us exceed our ability to comfortably meet them.

Much of the stress we experience is useful, and even enjoyable, in that it energizes us, challenges us, and helps us grow stronger. Think, for instance, of a runner pushing herself to go a little faster than is comfortable or a retiree enrolling in college decades after being in school.

While short-term or mild-intensity stress can be good for us, prolonged or intense stress is generally not. In fact, such stress is known to impair health, happiness, and productivity.

Researchers have shown, for example, that this type of stress can disrupt the immune system and contribute to cardiovascular disease. Stress can impair brain functions such as memory. In persons with chronic pain, stress tends to increase suffering. Stress makes it harder to resist addictive urges. Intense or prolonged stress can also reduce our ability to work efficiently and can decrease our sense of well-being.

Anxiety is the most common emotional response to intense or prolonged stress. Anxiety can be experienced in various ways:

- Worry

- Difficulty concentrating

- Feelings of fear

- Desire to avoid what is feared

- Distressing dreams associated with the fear

- Physical reactions such as muscle tension, sweating, and changes in breathing and heart rate

Anxiety isn't the only emotional response to prolonged or intense stress, however. *Depressed mood* and *irritability* are also common responses. For more information on how to deal with those responses to stress, please refer to Chapter 2, Mood Regulation, and Chapter 4, Anger and Frustration Management.

How to Recognize Stress

Change is generally a source of stress, so be on the lookout when your circumstances change in some way. Be especially on the lookout when the changes aren't under your control. Unwanted changes, such as illness or injury, are easily recognized as sources of stress. But even desired changes, such as a promotion at work or a new relationship, are also usually stressful.

Common sources of stress include the following:

- Injuries

- Illnesses

- Chronic pain

- Losses of important roles or identities, such as when no longer working

- Losses of loved ones

- Relationship problems

- Work demands

- Family demands

- Money problems

- Traffic, long lines, and other hassles

Symptoms that can signal excess stress include the following:

- Feeling overwhelmed

- Feeling anxious

- Having mood swings, including depression

- Feeling irritable and/or exhibiting anger outbursts

- Experiencing heart palpitations

- Feeling run down and tired

- Experiencing reduced sexual desire

- Developing muscle tension, headaches, stomach aches, back pain, or neck pain

- Having problems with attention and memory

Unhealthy behaviors often increase in times of stress. These can include the following:

- Overeating, unhealthy eating, or not eating

- Using excessive amounts of caffeinated beverages

- Smoking

- Consuming alcohol or other substances excessively

- Not exercising

- Not sleeping or resting enough, or sleeping too much

Complete the following worksheet to help you more fully understand your own stress and anxiety.

■ **Understanding Stress and Anxiety Worksheet**

Describe in your own words what *stress* is:

_____

_____

Describe in your own words what *anxiety* is:

_____

_____

List some other emotional responses, besides anxiety, that you and others might experience in times of prolonged or intense stress:

_____

_____

List some of the problems that can be caused by prolonged or intense stress:

_____

_____

List some sources of stress in your life:

_____

_____

List the symptoms that you tend to experience when stressed:

_____

_____

List some of your unhealthy stress-response behaviors:

_____

_____

In the following discussion you'll find descriptions of ways to lower stress and restore energy through techniques for relaxing the body and the mind.

Regular practice of one or more of these techniques will help you gain a sense of control over your personal experience of stress, anxiety, and tension. With these under better control, you'll have more energy and focus for making other positive changes in your life.

Keep in mind that these self-management techniques work better the more you practice them. Also be aware that it's best to practice these techniques during less stressful times until you become skilled enough to use them during times of high stress.

Use Your Body to Relax

Stress, anxiety, and tension can be regulated by changing what you do with your body. Here are some of the ways you can do this:

- **Relaxing your muscles**: You've probably noticed that stress, anxiety, and worry can cause you to tense up in certain parts of your body, such as your upper shoulders. Have you also noticed that relaxing your muscles can reduce stress, anxiety, and worry? This works like a two-way street in that your mind can influence what your muscles do, but your muscles can also influence what your mind does. So in order to calm your mind more effectively, one of the key skills is muscle relaxation.

  Try sitting or lying comfortably and consciously relaxing each of your muscle groups (e.g., starting at the head and working down the body). Pay special attention to common trouble spots, such as the forehead, jaw muscles, and shoulders. Smooth your forehead, unclench your jaw, put a slight smile on the corners of your mouth, and let your shoulders relax and drop into a more comfortable position.

  It's helpful to have spoken instructions as a guide while learning to use relaxation techniques. Many resources are available, some at no cost. For example, very high-quality audio instructions for relaxation can be downloaded via the Internet courtesy of Dartmouth College Health Services Student Health Promotion and Wellness:

https://www.dartmouth.edu/~healthed/relax/downloads. html#muscle.

Please note that the specific Internet links provided in this book are subject to change by their webmasters over time. Links were current at the time this book was written but may have changed by the time you read this chapter.

If you find a link is no longer working, just search for some of the key terms, and you'll generally find what you're looking for or something very similar. In this case, you could search for "Relaxation Downloads Dartmouth College." When you get to the Dartmouth site, select the download labeled "Progressive Muscle Relaxation." You'll also see options for other relaxation methods you might want to try, including those described next.

Muscle relaxation instructions often tell you to first deliberately tense your muscles and then relax them. While this seems paradoxical, the tense–relax technique is actually very helpful at producing deep relaxation, perhaps deeper than you've ever felt before. However, if you have a medical condition that makes it unhealthy or impossible to follow the tension instructions, just ignore those and follow the instructions to relax your muscles.

Relaxing your breathing: Many people have heard that taking deep breaths can help decrease stress and anxiety, and that's true. However, most people haven't been taught how to do it in the most helpful way.

The secret to relaxed breathing is to push your stomach outward as you inhale. This allows you to inflate your lungs more fully so you can breathe more slowly. Instead of breathing about 14 times a minute like most people, or about 18 times a minute like someone who's highly anxious, work toward a slower, more relaxed breathing rhythm of 6 to 10 times per minute.

Try to spend a little longer blowing the air out, as this is the most relaxing part of the breath cycle. Breathing in this way will turn down your body's fight-or-flight response system and allow you to relax more fully and let go of some tension.

Smartphone users can find helpful training apps for relaxed breathing, such as Breathe2Relax. Free relaxed-breathing audio training is available via numerous Internet sites, such as the previously mentioned Dartmouth website.

If you have medical problems that affect your ability to breathe deeply, talk with your healthcare providers about the use of this method of relaxation.

- **Exercising**: Regular exercise can reduce anxiety and tension and increase confidence and self-esteem. Plan a safe exercise program with the guidance of your healthcare providers to take into account any health or mobility limitations you have.

  The importance of regular exercise as a coping technique cannot be overemphasized, which is why it's mentioned in every chapter of this book. Even if you don't exercise regularly, getting out and walking or doing some other safe physical activity can help you relax during times of extra stress.

Use the following worksheet to help you understand and begin to practice these three ways of using your body to relax.

Relaxing your muscles

Describe how this method works:

_____

_____

Now try this method out for a few minutes and then report here what you did and what the experience was like for you:

_____

_____

Relaxing your breathing

Describe how this method works:

_____

_____

Now try this method out for a few minutes and then report here what you did and what the experience was like for you:

_____

_____

Exercising

Describe how this method works:

_____

_____

Now try this method out for a few minutes and then report here what you did and what the experience was like for you:

_____

_____

Stress, anxiety, and tension can also be regulated by changing what you do with your mind. Here are some of the ways you can do this:

- **Relaxing with mental imagery**: Once you've practiced the breathing and muscle relaxation exercises just described, you may want to try imagining yourself visiting a peaceful, pleasant location as a way to relax.

    Imagery typically works best with eyes closed and muscles relaxed. The place you visualize can be one that you've actually visited, one you've seen in a picture or a movie, or one you create by just using your imagination. Make this experience as real as possible by imagining as many details as you can.

    You might, for example, imagine stretching out in the soft warmth of a sandy beach while sunlight glistens on blue-green waves and palm trees sway and rustle in the tropical breeze.

    You might imagine breathing in the scent of ferns and wet earth as you recline on a mossy boulder and dip your foot or hand into the coolness of a gurgling brook that flows through a lush green meadow surrounded by towering redwoods.

    Or you might imagine being lulled into deep relaxation by the lapping of tiny waves against your canoe as you drift across a pond under the glow of a full moon while owls hoot and crickets chirp in the distance.

    Relax and enjoy your imagery for a while. When you're ready to leave, gradually bring your attention back to the room you're in. Slowly open your eyes and gently move your body, noticing the things around you as you end your relaxing mental imagery experience.

    As you're learning the imagery method of relaxation, you'll probably benefit from guided instruction from sources such as those mentioned earlier in the chapter. For example, the Dartmouth website https://www.dartmouth.edu/~healthed/relax/downloads.html has several guided imagery exercises.

Relaxing with meditation: Meditation is another powerful mental stress-reduction technique. While people have meditated for centuries, interest in this practice is growing as scientific study convincingly demonstrates its ability to improve physical and mental health and well-being.

One form of meditation involves silent repetition of a word, often called a "mantra." Sometimes Sanskrit words, such as *om*, are used, but English words, such as *relax* or *calm*, work just as well.

Meditation can be combined with the muscle relaxation and breathing methods just described. To try meditation, sit down, close your eyes, breathe slowly and deeply, relax your muscles, and silently repeat "relax" or another mantra each time you exhale.

Meditation isn't limited to focusing on a single word. You can, for example, meditate by focusing on short phrases, such as a prayer. Or you can meditate while focusing on mental images, for example picturing the air flowing in and out of your lungs.

Meditation also doesn't need to be done with eyes closed while sitting still and alone. You can learn to meditate while walking, swimming, or otherwise moving about. You can also meditate with others. Many yoga classes incorporate meditation practice along with physical exercise.

It's normal for your mind to wander to other topics as you meditate. When you notice this happening, gently bring your attention back to your breathing and mantra or other focus. With practice, your mind will gradually grow more skilled at remaining focused during meditation.

Practicing mindfulness: *Mindfulness* is a term for a type of meditation similar to that just described. However, mindfulness also incorporates an approach to life in general that involves greater awareness and appreciation of the *present moment*, rather than unproductive focus on the past or future. Mindfulness training also encourages adoption of an attitude of nonjudgmental observation as an alternative to emotional overreactivity.

Mindfulness training programs, such as Mindfulness-Based Stress Reduction (MBSR), have been shown in many research studies to have beneficial effects on health and well-being. For example, researchers have demonstrated measurable growth in important regions of the brain after just a few weeks of mindfulness meditation practice.

Free guided mindfulness meditation exercises are available via the Internet, for example by searching for the UCLA Mindful Awareness Research Center.

Smartphone and tablet apps and additional training in meditation and mindfulness are also available on the Internet at sites such as https://www.headspace.com and https://insighttimer.com.

Mindfulness meditation training programs are available in many communities. Such live instruction and the group support that goes along with it are generally best at motivating participants to practice meditation enough to make it a long-term habit.

Use the following worksheet to help you understand and begin to practice the mental relaxation methods described here.

Relaxing with mental imagery

Describe how this method works:

_____

_____

Now try this method out for a few minutes and then report here what you did and what the experience was like for you:

_____

_____

Relaxing with meditation

Describe how this method works:

_____

_____

Now try this method out for a few minutes and then report here what you did and what the experience was like for you:

_____

_____

Practicing mindfulness

Describe how this method works:

_____

_____

Now try this method out for a few minutes and then report here what you did and what the experience was like for you:

_____

_____

_____

Frequently, stress is the result of taking on more tasks than you have the time or other resources to accomplish. Stress management therefore requires careful examination and prioritization of goals. Goals toward the bottom of the priority list may need to be let go.

Often after an injury or illness, or just with advancing age, it takes longer to accomplish what you used to accomplish. With chronic pain, it's generally smart to slow down and pace yourself. When you're taking reasonable steps to slow down and pace yourself, you naturally have to cut back on what you try to accomplish. For these reasons, prioritizing goals, as well as eliminating some of them, is even more important for those dealing with injury, illness, aging, or pain.

If you feel overwhelmed by responsibilities at work or at home, take some time to prioritize goals and consult with your supervisor or family members to set more realistic expectations.

Also examine your goals to see which of them could be delegated to someone else. Is there anyone kind enough and capable enough to help you out if you ask them? Can you afford to pay for help? If you just didn't do something, would someone else step in and take care of it?

In addition to prioritizing goals and delegating and eliminating some of them, it's also smart to manage stress by subdividing big goals into smaller ones. Breaking bigger goals into smaller steps can help you feel a sense of accomplishment as you complete each step.

Making to-do lists can also help to organize and manage your responsibilities.

Chapter 1, Self-Management: Changing Behavior and Thoughts, contains more guidance on some of these prioritization and goal-subdividing skills, and you're encouraged to go back and review it now.

Once you've reviewed that chapter, come back here and complete the following worksheet to improve your skills at prioritizing and subdividing goals.

List the tasks, big or small, that are on your to-do list:

_____

_____

_____

_____

Now go back and review that list to find one or more tasks that are not absolutely essential. Draw a line through that task or those tasks. Write down the goal(s) you decided to let go of here:

_____

_____

_____

_____

Now pick one or more tasks you can delegate to someone else and write down the task(s) and the person(s) you delegate them to here:

_____

_____

_____

_____

Pick one or more of the bigger tasks from your list on the previous page and use the space below to break the bigger task(s) into smaller tasks:

_____

_____

_____

_____

_____

_____

_____

Excess stress tends to cause anxiety, and one of the most common and least pleasant features of anxiety is worry about the future.

A little worry can be helpful in that it prompts us to plan for how we'll deal with potential bad outcomes. Too much worry, though, is just unpleasant and unproductive. Fortunately, prolonged or repetitive worry can be regulated somewhat by actively controlling what we choose to focus on.

Even though it seems hard to stop a worrying train of thought, you can have some success with techniques such as changing where you are and what you're doing. For example, to interrupt worry, you might do one or more of the following:

- Switch to a different task

- Talk to a friend

- Change your location

- Go for a walk

- Turn on the TV

- Open a book or magazine.

- Tell yourself forcefully to "stop" the worry and then deliberately think about something else

You can also try adopting the mindfulness perspective described earlier in this chapter. When a worry crosses your mind, just acknowledge it as a fleeting thought, let it pass through your mind without judgment, and then return your focus to the present.

Not all worry is a waste of time. Sometimes worry generates solutions to real problems. However, it can help to schedule a designated worry time (e.g., 10 or 15 minutes set aside at a certain time each day).

When worry topics come up at other times, tell yourself that you'll deal with them later. If necessary, jot the topic down so you won't worry about forgetting it. A pad of paper by the bedside can be helpful for jotting down worrisome thoughts that might otherwise keep you awake at night.

Structuring worry times as suggested here gives you more sense of control, which itself tends to lower stress. Paradoxically, some people find that the intensity of their worry lessens when they deliberately try to worry during their designated worry time.

Use the following worksheet to improve your skills at managing worry.

■ Choose When and How to Worry Worksheet

In your own words, state how some worry can be useful:

_____

_____

_____

List some ways that you can interrupt excessive worry:

_____

_____

_____

Describe what is meant by scheduling a "worry time" and how this can be helpful:

_____

_____

_____

Now try scheduling a "worry time" on at least one day and come back here and describe what happened:

_____

_____

_____

_____

Describe a technique you can try if worry disrupts your sleep at night:

_____

_____

_____

Put the Situation into Perspective

Excess worry and stress often come from *overestimating the danger in a situation*. This overestimation can take one of two forms:

■ Thinking the likelihood of the feared event actually happening is greater than it really is, or

■ Thinking the feared event will be worse than it really is.

Psychologists call such overestimation of danger "catastrophizing." To catastrophize less, stop and think:

■ What's the likelihood of this feared event actually happening?

■ If the feared event actually happens, how terrible will it really be?

Often, the answer to these questions will help to lower worry and stress. For example, possible answers to these questions might include the following:

■ If I fail at this task, it will seem important today, but in the big picture it's really not that important. In a year or two, this will probably be just a distant memory.

■ If this person doesn't like or respect me, it's not the end of the world. No one is liked and respected by everyone.

■ The odds of this plane (car) crashing on this particular flight (trip) are less than one in a million, so why waste time worrying?

As these examples show, the thoughts you choose to focus on can lower the intensity of your worry and stress. Focusing on positive coping statements, instead of adopting a helpless attitude, can reduce worry and stress. Here are some more examples of helpful, stress-reducing thoughts:

■ I've survived many tough situations, and each one has made me stronger. I'll get through this one and end up even stronger.

■ Even though I'm not perfect, I still love and accept myself. Perfection is an unrealistic and unhealthy goal.

- There are many possible explanations for this symptom. I'll get it checked out, but in the meantime, I won't catastrophize about it.

- It's normal to feel fear in this situation; I'll just practice my relaxation techniques to reduce the fear.

- Fear is just an emotion that will pass.

- Avoiding fearful situations will make my fears stronger, but facing my fears will eventually reduce their power over me.

Use the following worksheet to increase your skill at managing worry and stress by putting situations into perspective.

What are the two types of catastrophizing described in this section?

Type 1:

_____

_____

Type 2:

_____

_____

Think of an example of worry caused by overestimating the likelihood of danger.

Write the example here:

_____

_____

Now write a more adaptive way of talking to yourself about that situation:

_____

_____

Think of an example of worry caused by overestimating how bad the outcome will be.

Write the example here:

_____

_____

Now write a more adaptive way of talking to yourself about that situation:

_____

_____

Avoid Avoidance

It's natural to want to avoid activities, people, places, or things that trigger a stress response. For example, many people who have been in serious auto accidents feel fearful about traffic and try to avoid motor vehicle transportation.

In the short term, avoidance works well. If you avoid something that scares you, your fear will temporarily decrease. In the auto accident example, if you have a driving phobia and get off the freeway when you feel fear, your level of fear will usually decrease almost immediately. In the long term, however, this strategy actually causes the phobia to worsen. The more you avoid what you fear, the stronger the fear becomes.

Just like the cowboy who wisely gets right back on the horse after it throws him off, the person who wants to overcome anxiety is better off confronting the feared situation.

As Ralph Waldo Emerson once said:

Do the thing you fear and the death of fear is certain.

This is one of those cases in which doing what feels good, namely avoidance, isn't always good for you. Following an auto accident, for example, you'll be better off rationally deciding whether it's in your best interest to resume driving rather than letting fear be your guide.

If you rationally decide that avoidance is not a good long-term solution, then gradually re-exposing yourself to the feared situation will help prevent the fear response from becoming a long-term problem.

Some persons with a newly acquired disability that is visible to others feel self-conscious and try to manage their social anxiety by avoiding going out in public. This avoidance, however, doesn't solve the problem and can lead to other difficulties, such as depressed mood that can come from social isolation.

The more adaptive approach is generally to push yourself to get out in public, recognizing that self-consciousness is likely to gradually decrease over time. It may help to spend some time out in public with other persons with similar visible signs of disability who have already learned to feel comfortable around others. Numerous people who use wheelchairs or prosthetic limbs have reported this type of experience to be helpful.

It's also useful to watch what you are thinking as you get used to being in public situations. For example, rather than assuming that children or other strangers who look at you are being critical, consider the likelihood that they are just curious. Even if a stranger happens, by chance, to think critical thoughts, how important to your long-term well-being is that one person's opinion?

Use the following worksheet to help you understand avoidance and learn how to deal with it better.

■ Avoid Avoidance Worksheet

Explain what Ralph Waldo Emerson meant when he said, "Do the thing you fear and the death of fear is certain":

_____

_____

_____

_____

_____

List one or more activities you've been avoiding out of fear:

_____

_____

_____

_____

Pick at least one activity you've been avoiding out of fear that you are ready to confront. Write your plan for gradually confronting your fear by reducing your avoidance:

_____

_____

_____

_____

_____

_____

_____

_____

_____

_____

Chapter 4   *Anger and Frustration Management*

Humans probably wouldn't be so good at getting angry if anger didn't serve some valuable purposes. Anger can energize us, inspire and motivate us to push back against injustice, and give us strength and courage to fight for the lives of our loved ones and for ourselves.

But anger has its downside and is one of those things in life that's best enjoyed in moderation. Here are some of the harmful effects of anger:

- Within our bodies, chronic anger increases the risk of high blood pressure, stroke, heart disease, gastric ulcers, and bowel disease. Anger may also increase the risk of some types of cancer.

- Chronic or intense anger can have toxic effects on relationships, leading to emotional and sometimes physical wounds.

- And on a more national and global scale, intense anger helps to fuel political division, hatred, war, and genocide.

Anger management skills are valuable for everyone to develop, but especially valuable for persons who are adjusting to injury, illness, pain, age-related changes in ability, or any combination of these. These life changes can be frustrating and stressful, making it easier for anger reactions to be triggered.

When abilities decline, the help of others may be needed more, and the failure of others to meet this need provides more opportunity for frustration and anger.

Also, the depressed mood and pain that often accompany a decline in ability make it easier for anger to be triggered.

Therefore, it's important to develop awareness of anger triggers and practice some of the following strategies to reduce frustration and anger.

Taking a time-out when frustrated or annoyed is one of the simplest but most effective ways to prevent anger reactions. Depending on the situation, this may involve either slowly counting to 10 or 20 before responding or temporarily stopping the interaction and moving to a different location in order to regain composure and perspective.

If you're planning to try this strategy with family members, coworkers, or close friends, it's a good idea to let them know ahead of time. You can explain what you'll be doing by saying something like this:

> "I'm working on keeping my cool better when I get frustrated. One thing I'm trying is called 'time-out.' This means taking a break to calm down and gather my thoughts before I react in anger. When I do this, I'll sometimes just count to 10 or 20 before I react. Other times, when I need a longer break to calm down, I'll walk away.
>
> "I'm doing this because I don't want to say or do anything hurtful. You can help by allowing me to take this time-out to calm myself down before we continue the discussion. And if you ever feel our discussions are getting too heated, I hope you'll also feel free to call a time-out.
>
> "Is it okay with you if we try this out, and do you have any questions for me?"

This explanation will help to keep them from interpreting your silence or walking away as a sign that you don't care. Letting them know ahead of time will also decrease the chance that they'll interrupt your time-out by following you or trying to continue the discussion before you're ready to resume.

As soon as you've calmed down, let the other person know that you're calling a "time-in" and ask if it's okay to continue the discussion.

Use the following worksheet to develop a plan for trying out the time-out method of frustration and anger management.

▓ Time-Out Worksheet

List one or more situations in which you want to try the time-out frustration and anger management technique:

_____

_____

_____

Write down a few sentences as a script for how you'll tell the other person or persons ahead of time what you're doing when you take a time-out so they don't misunderstand:

_____

_____

_____

Write down a plan for what you'll do with your body during the time-out to calm down, such as relaxing your muscles, breathing slowly, smiling, or taking a walk:

_____

_____

_____

Write down some alternate ways of thinking about the situation to help calm yourself down, such as finding humor in the situation, trying to see the other person's perspective, or adopting the nonjudgmental attitude discussed in the section "Use Your Mind to Relax" in Chapter 3, Stress and Anxiety Management:

_____

_____

_____

_____

_____

_____

For many of us, the most effective way to reduce frustration and anger is to change the way we think about things. As you may recall from Chapter 2, Mood Regulation, our thoughts play a major role in determining our emotions. In many respects, anger reactions are not a direct result of other people's actions; they are instead a result of how we think about their actions. Specifically, anger arises in us when we think in ways that are not fully realistic.

Unrealistic expectations are the most common anger triggers. When we expect others to behave in a way that's different from how they actually behave, we set ourselves up to become frustrated, irritated, or outright angry. Likewise, unrealistic expectations of ourselves can set us up for self-directed frustration, irritation, or anger.

In most cases, we'll have more success in changing our expectations than in changing other people's behavior. So, one of the most powerful ways to reduce anger is to work on developing more realistic expectations.

The unrealistic expectations that tend to trigger anger usually involve words such as the following:

- *Should* (e.g., They should do it my way.)

- *Right* (e.g., That's not right.)

- *Fair* (e.g., It's not fair.)

- *Must* (e.g., You must do as I say.)

Even though we may feel that our personal rules and expectations are entirely reasonable, the reality is that they aren't shared by everyone else. When our rules or expectations are violated, we tend to react with anger. Such anger can be reduced by changing our expectations or "*should* thoughts."

The first step is to become aware of when we're having these expectations or *should* thoughts that lead to anger. Then we can substitute more realistic and tolerant thoughts. Examples of more realistic and tolerant thoughts include the following:

- It would be nice if everybody shared my (driving skills/ wisdom/values/good manners/political views), but they just don't.

- It's not realistic to expect people to understand my disability until I've educated them about it, and even then, a lot of people are slow learners.

- It takes all kinds.

- Oh well.

- Whatever.

- It is what it is.

- Nobody's perfect, including me.

- We all have quirks.

- We're all just trying to get by the best we can.

- Perhaps common decency isn't so common after all.

- It's not really my job to police the world.

- I've got to expect 49% of people to be below average—that's just basic statistics.

- I like it when people respect me, but there's no law that says they have to.

- I do nice things because I want to, not because I expect anything in return.

- I don't like this situation, but it's not under my control. I'll just bring it to the attention of a supervisor and not stress over it.

- Wow! That's some terrible customer service. But it's a free country. She's free to give lousy service, and I'm free to (leave no tip/take my business elsewhere/let her boss know/write an equally terrible online review).

- Sometimes bad things happen to good people. That's just the way it is.

- *Que sera, sera* (Whatever will be, will be).

- *C'est la vie* (That's life).

- An old one that parents often try to teach: Life isn't always fair.

- And a new one from popular culture: Haters gonna hate.

We can express our wishes and preferences, but recognize that, in most cases, people have the option to disregard them.

Of course, some *should* thoughts are useful, especially when the situation is one we actually have some control over, a law or formal contract is being broken, or someone is in danger. In such cases, assertively communicating our expectations or calling upon appropriate authorities may well be a reasonable course of action. Assertive communication skills are covered in the next section of this chapter.

Regarding the concept of *fairness*, it's important to recognize that judgments of fairness depend on one's point of view. Two rational people can view a situation from different perspectives and come up with different opinions about what's fair.

For example, from one perspective, it might seem fair that everyone should pay the same income tax rate. After all, isn't everyone being treated the same the very essence of fairness?

But from another perspective, it might seem fair to correct for huge income and wealth inequality by taxing the ultra-wealthy more heavily. After all, doesn't it seem unfair when an executive is paid a thousand times more than a hard-working factory employee?

Rather than fixating on the concept of fairness and becoming angered by a perceived lack of fairness, it's often wiser to step back and think instead in terms of what would be best overall for society. We can figure out what our true values are, and act and vote based on them, without unhealthy chronic anger or resentment.

Regarding the concept of *rights*, it helps to be mindful of the distinction between enforceable legal rights and our own perceptions about what seems good or proper. For example, some people believe they have a "right" to be treated at all times with respect or courtesy, when in reality, in certain situations, this may just be their preference.

We can feel free to not associate with people who don't show respect or courtesy toward us and to inform their supervisor if they have one, but we don't need to get unnecessarily worked up by confusing preferences for enforceable legal rights.

Keep in mind, though, that many countries have specific laws that establish enforceable rights for persons with disabilities. The website of the Disability Rights Education & Defense Fund (http://dredf.org) lists relevant laws by country. In the United States, the *Americans with Disabilities Act* provides important legal protections. More information about these legal rights and about self-advocacy can be found at the Equal Rights Center (http://www.equalrightscenter.org).

If you're one of the over four million parents with a disability in the United States, the *Parents with Disabilities Toolkit* provides a summary of disability laws that protect families' rights. This is a free publication jointly developed by the Christopher & Dana Reeve Foundation (https://www.christopherreeve.org) and the National Council of Disability (http://ncd.gov), both of which are excellent resources for additional disability-related information.

Over the next few days, be alert to situations in which you feel frustrated, annoyed, or outright angry, and pay attention to what thoughts or expectations fuel this reaction. Use the following worksheet to help you become more aware of your *should* thoughts and to develop more adaptive ways of thinking about those situations.

■ *Should* **Thoughts Worksheet**

Think of a recent situation in which you felt irritated, and answer the following questions:

What happened?

_____

_____

_____

What *should* thoughts fueled your anger?

_____

_____

_____

What alternate thoughts could you try next time to reduce your anger reaction?

_____

_____

_____

Take three self-sticking notes or other small pieces of paper and write on each a short phrase to remind yourself to watch out for *should* thoughts. For example, you might write the word *Should* with a line drawn through it, followed by the words *It would be nice if...* Place each note in a location where you'll see it often or where you tend to become irritated. For example, if you tend to become angry at bad drivers, you might attach the note to your car keys so you'll be reminded about *should* thoughts before you start your car. Come back and report here what words you wrote and where you placed your reminders:

_____

_____

_____

_____

_____

_____

While *should* thoughts are the main fuel for most anger, two other unrealistic types of thought are also important to learn to recognize. One of these is a tendency to *take other people's behavior personally*, as in: "They deliberately did that just to irritate me."

It's true that occasionally people really do mean to offend or annoy us, but often they don't. They may just be unfriendly or unhelpful because they're having a bad day or a bad life. They may just really enjoy loud conversation or loud music without specifically intending to upset us. They may be honking or waving obscene gestures at someone else. They may even have hit the car horn by accident.

Being able to step back and think about other possible reasons for the person's behavior helps us to not automatically feel personally attacked. And when we don't feel personally attacked, we're less likely to respond in anger.

By stepping back for a moment, sometimes we may even be able to use our power of empathy to understand a bit about the person's motivation. If we can put ourselves in the offending person's shoes, we may be able to feel a little less offended.

Here are some examples of things we can say to ourselves to take annoying behavior less personally and try to feel some empathy for the other person:

- Maybe he's just having a bad day.

- Maybe she didn't mean it personally.

- She's got a miserable job. Who's to say I'd do any better?

- He probably doesn't know any better.

- Maybe she wasn't raised to see things the way I see things.

- Maybe he's just really insecure.

- They're probably under stress and doing the best they can right now.

- And an old saying attributed by some to Plato and by others to Scottish minister John Watson: Be kind, for everyone you meet is fighting a hard battle.

The other type of unrealistic thinking that fuels anger is *exaggeration of danger or harm*. People sometimes call this "making a mountain out of a mole hill." As you may recall from Chapter 3, Stress and Anxiety Management, psychologists sometimes call this "catastrophizing." The tendency to exaggerate danger or harm can fuel both anxiety and anger.

As an example of how this type of thinking can lead to unproductive anger reactions, I'll share an incident from my childhood. My dog and I were playing on our front lawn when she wandered over to inspect the neighbors' decorative fountain. Before I could call her back, the boy next door squirted something on my dog's back, announcing with a sadistic grin that the liquid was "pool acid."

I must have recently seen a television show in which a person was dissolved in or disfigured by acid, since I instantly imagined acid eating a hole through my dog's back. Because this catastrophic thinking triggered an immediate rage response, I neglected to stop and notice that my dog wasn't yelping in pain. I also failed to consider rinsing the "pool acid" off her back.

Instead, I darted across the lawn and leapt upon my neighbor's back with all the fury I could muster. Fortunately for him, the destructive power of my skinny, 7-year-old body matched that of his "pool acid," and his back ended up as unscathed as my dog's.

When adults have the same kind of overreaction, however, the results are not always so benign. Overestimation of danger or harm contributes to some of the anger and fear that drive groups apart today.

Clever political leaders, media pundits, and business promoters sometimes encourage overestimation of danger or harm as a way to win elections, drum up support for policies or military actions, increase ratings, or sell more products. If you find yourself frequently becoming angered and frightened by what you watch, listen to, or read, think about whether those delivering these upsetting messages might be trying to shape your opinions to serve their own purposes. Before allowing yourself to be riled up in this way, stop and make a realistic assessment of how great the danger or harm really is. Be wary of claims that some group is out to "take over," "ruin," "destroy," or "wage war" against your favorite institutions or way of life. In other words, think critically before being manipulated into grabbing your torch and pitchfork.

There are, of course, some genuine dangers and situations in which decisive action is warranted, but first consider the actual evidence and the possible motivations of those who might benefit from your anger and fear.

Overestimation of danger or harm also results in unnecessary anger in everyday personal interactions. Yes, you may not like what someone has done, but stop and ask yourself if it's really dangerous or harmful enough to warrant an angry reaction.

Even if a situation really is dangerous or harmful, wouldn't you generally be better off focusing on solutions rather than wasting time reacting in anger? Here are some more examples of what you might say to yourself to avoid overreacting in this way:

- Will this really seem that important a year or two from now?

- It's not a life-or-death mistake.

- I don't like it, but it's not the end of the world.

- Is it possible that it's not as bad as it seems?

- Even situations that seem bad often have a "silver lining."

- Let's focus on finding solutions.

- It's unfortunate, but I'll just make the best of it.

- I'll just use this to make myself stronger.

- Is someone trying to manipulate me into overreacting?

- Does this person who's trying to get me scared and angry have a hidden agenda?

- Do I really need to feel so threatened when someone (looks at/talks to) my (girlfriend/wife/boyfriend/husband/partner)? Isn't our relationship stronger than that? Maybe I can just take it as a compliment that so many people find (her or him) attractive.

- Is it really worth going to jail or the hospital over this?

- Does it really cause me so much harm when someone (insults me, insults my family, insults my team, makes an obscene gesture, or shows disrespect) that I have to respond aggressively?

- And the old classic from childhood: Sticks and stones will break my bones, but names will never hurt me.

Assertive Communication

Another important way to reduce anger and frustration is to practice assertive communication. *Assertiveness* refers to a way of communicating that takes the middle ground between being passive and being aggressive.

Assertive communication involves expressing your preferences, feelings, and thoughts in a clear, direct, and respectful way. Assertiveness means standing up for yourself without bullying others or putting others down. Assertiveness can include educating others about rights or accommodations you are entitled to because of a disability.

When people communicate too passively and allow themselves to be manipulated or verbally run over by others, they often feel resentful. Holding anger or resentment inside may lead to unhealthy physical and psychological consequences.

Sometimes bottled-up anger bursts out in uncontrolled ways, resulting in behavior that is later regretted. Thus, people who communicate too passively can also occasionally be outwardly aggressive.

People with passive communication styles frequently express their anger in subtle ways, such as being late or "forgetting" to do something for the person at whom they're angry. This is termed *passive aggression*, as it involves getting back at others in an indirect or timid way. Usually, however, such indirect forms of aggression just irritate the other person and unnecessarily perpetuate a hostile, unpleasant pattern of interaction.

The more adaptive approach for persons with passive communication styles to take is to practice speaking up assertively for what they like or don't like. Assertive communicators make requests for what they want. They also set limits, or just say "no," when feeling pressured to meet demands that aren't reasonable.

In comparison to aggressive communication, assertive communication involves less emphasis on winning or losing and more on finding workable solutions for both parties.

Replacing aggressiveness with assertiveness involves

- speaking in softer tones, while still being firm and clear,

- listening to and trying to understand the other person's point of view, and

- avoiding threats or bullying behaviors.

To decrease the chance that others will react defensively, assertive communicators frequently use *I* statements. This term refers to a way of phrasing observations or requests in the first person. *You* statements, by contrast, are more likely to lead to defensive reactions. Picture, for example, a conversation in which you've been asked to do something you don't have time to do.

You could respond with a *you* statement such as, "You are being too demanding." This type of *you* statement generally leaves the listener feeling judged in a negative way and, therefore, defensive. The conversation typically then deteriorates from there.

Responding with an *I* statement often turns out better because it doesn't elicit such a defensive reaction. You might say, for example, "I hear what you're asking, and I know it's very important to you, but I simply don't have time to get that done this week. Can we talk about another plan?"

As another example, picture a situation in which you're having trouble getting your point across to your supervisor at work when you're requesting a reasonable accommodation for your disability. You might be tempted to blurt out in frustration, "You're not listening to me!" Such a statement could easily lead to defensive denial: "Yes, I am!" If you instead say, "I'm not feeling heard," this *I* statement is less likely to lead to an unproductive argument and more likely to lead to a renewed effort at understanding.

In assertively advocating for rights, access, or accommodations as a person with a disability, it can sometimes be helpful to join forces with others. For example, if wheelchair access at a new restaurant is poor, the owner may be more likely to make changes in response to a letter signed by several customers than one signed by a single person. As noted in the previous section, more information on disability rights advocacy is available at the Equal Rights Center (http://www.equalrightscenter.org).

Use the two worksheets that follow to think about ways you can increase your assertive communication.

■ **Assertiveness Worksheet for Reducing Aggressive Communication**

Observe your interactions over the next few days and try to identify at least one episode of aggressive communication. Describe the episode(s) below and write down some ideas about how you could handle similar situations in the future more assertively.

What was the situation?

_____

_____

_____

_____

How did you handle the situation?

_____

_____

_____

_____

_____

How did the other person respond?

_____

_____

_____

_____

How could you have communicated more assertively?

_____

_____

_____

_____

_____

■ **Assertiveness Worksheet for Reducing Passive Communication**

Observe your interactions over the next few days and try to identify at least one episode of passive communication. Describe the episode(s) below and write down some ideas about how you could handle similar situations in the future more assertively.

What was the situation?

_____

_____

_____

_____

_____

How did you handle the situation?

_____

_____

_____

_____

How did the other person respond?

_____

_____

_____

_____

How could you have communicated more assertively?

_____

_____

_____

_____

Anger reactions happen more easily when we're tired or hungry or otherwise not in our best condition. Therefore, it's important to consistently obtain sufficient sleep, regularly consume healthy food and beverages, exercise frequently, take medications as prescribed, manage stress, and avoid substance abuse. Think about some recent times you've been irritable. Did any of these conditions apply when you felt irritable?

- Were you tired?

- Were you hungry?

- Had you not been following a healthy diet?

- Had you not been drinking enough water or other healthy liquids?

- Had you not been exercising regularly?

- Had you not been taking prescribed medications regularly?

- Had you not been managing your stress by limiting how much you were trying to do?

- Had you not been managing your stress by practicing relaxation techniques?

- Were you using alcohol or drugs at the time of the anger reaction?

- Were you going through withdrawal from alcohol or drugs at the time of the anger reaction?

- If you regularly use legal stimulants such as nicotine (e.g., from smoking) or caffeine (e.g., from drinking coffee), were you starting to go through withdrawal?

For each factor that you think may contribute to you becoming angry, write down a plan for dealing with it on the following worksheet.

Sleep:

_____

_____

Nutrition (eating enough healthy food):

_____

_____

Hydration (drinking enough healthy fluids):

_____

_____

Exercise:

_____

_____

Medication:

_____

_____

Stress:

_____

_____

Substance use:

_____

_____

Relaxation is another helpful tool for managing frustration and anger. When our muscles are relaxed, the corners of our mouths are turned up in a slight smile, and we're breathing slowly and deeply, we're less likely to feel angry.

Before continuing, you may want to go back and review Chapter 3, Stress and Anxiety Management, to refresh your memory of the relaxation skills that work well for you. Some of these skills are summarized below:

- **Relaxing your muscles**: Consciously relax each of your muscle groups (e.g., starting at the head and working down the body). Pay special attention to common tension locations, including the forehead, jaw muscles, hands, and shoulders. Smooth your forehead, unclench your jaw and fists, put a slight smile on the corners of your mouth, and let your shoulders relax and drop into a more comfortable position.

- **Relaxing your breathing**: Breathe slowly and deeply, remembering to push your stomach outward as you inhale. This allows you to inflate your lungs more fully, so you can breathe more slowly.

  Instead of breathing about 14 times a minute like most people, or about 18 times a minute like someone who's stressed or angry, work toward a slower, more relaxed breathing rhythm of 6 to 10 times per minute. Try to spend a little longer blowing the air out, as this is the most relaxing part of the breath cycle.

  Breathing in this way will turn down your body's fight-or-flight response system and allow you to relax more fully and let go of some of the anger.

- **Relaxing with mental imagery**: Anger can also be calmed by imagining yourself in a peaceful and beautiful place or by picturing someone who brings out feelings of calmness and happiness.

Imagery typically works best when you're relaxed with your eyes closed. With practice, though, you might become good enough at mental imagery to go to your "happy place" with your eyes open in order to deal with frustrating situations in the moment, like the classic movie character Happy Gilmore.

The place you visualize can be one that you've actually visited, one you've seen in a picture or movie, or one you create by just using your imagination. Some people imagine visiting a beach or a peaceful river or lake.

Make this experience as real as possible by imagining as many details as you can. For example, imagine the look of the sky and the other things around you, the enjoyable scents and sounds you notice, and the pleasant temperature of the air around you. Relax in this place for a while and enjoy your visit.

When you're ready to leave your imaginary place, gradually bring your attention back to the room you're in. Slowly open your eyes and gently move your body, noticing the things around you as you end your relaxing mental imagery experience.

- **Relaxing with meditation**: Meditation is another mental stress-reduction technique that can help to replace anger with calmness.

One form of meditation involves silent repetition of a word or short phrase, often called a "mantra." Sometimes Sanskrit words, such as *om*, are used, but English words, such as *relax* or *calm*, work as well.

This practice can be combined with the slow, deep-breathing exercise just described. With your eyes closed and muscles relaxed, silently repeat "relax" or another mantra each time you exhale.

Don't be surprised or frustrated when your mind wanders to other topics as you meditate; this is normal. When you notice this happening, gently bring your attention back to your breathing and mantra. With practice, your mind will grow more skilled at remaining focused during meditation.

■ **Practicing mindfulness**: As you may recall from Chapter 3, Stress and Anxiety Management, *mindfulness* is both a type of meditation and an approach to life in general that involves awareness and appreciation of the present moment, rather than unproductive focus on the past or future.

Mindfulness training encourages a relaxed attitude of acceptance and nonjudgmental observation as an alternative to anger or other emotional overreactivity.

A mindful approach to anger involves observing any angry emotions, bodily sensations, thoughts, and images as they come up and allowing them to pass through awareness without acting reflexively on them.

A mindful perspective makes it easier to endure the temporary discomfort of anger, knowing that these emotions, sensations, thoughts, and images will pass. The focus on the present moment emphasized by mindfulness helps to reduce the anger that comes from preoccupation with upsetting events from the past.

Mindfulness training programs, such as Mindfulness Based Stress Reduction (MBSR), have been shown in many research studies to have beneficial effects on physical health and emotional well-being.

Apps and additional training in meditation and mindfulness are available on the Internet (e.g., https://www.headspace.com and https://insighttimer.com), and training programs are available in many communities.

Now try to recall some recent times you've been irritable and what your body was doing at the time. If you can't recall what your body was doing in past episodes, try to be aware during your next few episodes of anger. Or you might want to ask someone who knows you well what your body does when you're irritated.

Do your shoulders tighten or hunch up? Do you frown or tense up your forehead? Do you clench your jaw or fists? Is your breathing rapid or shallow?

For each tension factor that you think may contribute to irritability, write down a plan for dealing with it on the following worksheet.

For any of the following signs of tension that you exhibit when you're angry, write down a plan for how you'll become more aware of that behavior and what you'll do to relax instead.

Shoulder tension:

Example response: I know that I tend to get angry when I drive, so I'll put a self-sticking note on my dash where I'll see it when I get in the car. I'll write the word *shoulders* on it to remind myself to keep my shoulders relaxed because this will help me stay calm.

_____

_____

_____

_____

Forehead tension or frown:

_____

_____

_____

_____

Clenched jaw or fists:

_____

_____

_____

_____

Rapid or shallow breathing:

_____

_____

_____

_____

Humor is another powerful tool for reducing frustration, irritation, and annoyance. Humor is effective because it lightens mood and shifts perspective. It's hard to feel much anger while smiling or laughing.

Humor allows us to pause before reacting in a way that might escalate conflict. Sometimes humor helps us see the bigger picture and realize that what seemed really offensive might not actually be worth getting so upset about.

If you're not naturally good at using humor to defuse anger, it may help to develop friendships with those who do have a knack for making light of tense situations. At the same time, you might think about reducing contact with people who don't have much sense of humor and who seem chronically frustrated or resentful.

Of course, it's important to remember not to use humor in ways that will hurt others or cause them to react in anger. When it comes to expressing your amusement outwardly, it's usually better to laugh at yourself or the situation than to laugh at the other person. While feeling amused at the other person can be an effective antidote to anger, that amusement is best savored in private.

Do you have any favorite humorous recollections from the entertainment world or from real life that reliably bring a smile to your face? If so, you may want to pick one or two of these recollections to draw upon for comic relief during tense times to keep your temper in check.

Use the following worksheet to make yourself more aware of opportunities to use humor as a way to calm or prevent angry reactions.

■ Humor Worksheet

Over the next few days, look for situations in which those around you in real life, or characters on television or in movies, use humor to reduce or prevent anger. Summarize what you saw here:

_____

_____

_____

_____

_____

_____

_____

Also observe situations in which you either did or could have used humor to reduce or prevent your own anger. Summarize what happened and how you might improve your use of humor next time:

_____

_____

_____

_____

_____

_____

Write one or two favorite humorous scenes from your life or from the entertainment world that you can draw on for comic relief in tense situations in the future:

_____

_____

_____

_____

_____

_____

Greater peace of mind can often be achieved by a conscious decision to let go of anger and to cultivate a sense of forgiveness. There's an element of choice in whom we remain angry with and whom we forgive.

Forgiveness doesn't require that we approve of the other party's behavior. Forgiveness really just means that we're taking care of ourselves by not harboring unhealthy resentment.

If we choose to forgive, there is also no requirement that we communicate our forgiveness to those who hurt us or to associate with them in any other way. It may be perfectly rational to choose to minimize contact with certain people who have harmed us.

Forgiving also doesn't require that we forget what was done. We can learn lessons and work to make sure we don't end up in similar situations again without having to burden ourselves with chronic anger.

There are many reasons people do hurtful things, and we often won't understand exactly why. It can help, though, to try to see from other people's perspective why they did what they did. Were they, for example,

- lacking in awareness,

- poor at impulse control,

- acting out of fear or hurt, or

- just flawed human beings doing the best they could think of doing at the time?

Understanding why someone offends or hurts us can help us to forgive, but it isn't necessary to understand. We can simply say to ourselves something like this:

> Whatever reason they had, their hurtful act was probably what they saw as the best choice for them at the time. I choose to forgive them because I don't want to poison myself with anger.

Valuable additional guidance on how to forgive, as well as impressive outcome research, can be found by searching the Internet for The

Stanford Forgiveness Project and the psychologist who cofounded it, Dr. Fred Luskin.

Use the two worksheets that follow to think through your reactions to someone in your past and someone in your present toward whom you feel anger or resentment.

Forgiveness Worksheet for Anger at Persons in Your Past

List a person or persons from your past whom you haven't forgiven for something hurtful they said or did:

_____

_____

_____

_____

_____

Think about and write down some possible reasons for what they said or did:

_____

_____

_____

_____

Write down some reasons why it would be good for you to let go of anger toward them:

_____

_____

_____

_____

Write some specific thoughts you can repeat in your head to promote greater forgiveness:

_____

_____

_____

_____

_____

_____

■ Forgiveness Worksheet for Anger at Persons in Your Present

List a person or persons presently in your life whom you haven't forgiven for something hurtful they said or did or are currently doing:

_____

_____

_____

_____

_____

Think about and write down some possible reasons for what they said or did or are currently doing:

_____

_____

_____

_____

Write down some reasons why it would be good for you to let go of anger toward them:

_____

_____

_____

_____

_____

Write some specific thoughts you can repeat in your head to promote greater forgiveness:

_____

_____

_____

_____

_____

Anger often functions as a shield we put up to protect against acknowledgment of emotions that leave us feeling vulnerable. These vulnerable emotions include hurt, worry, jealousy, envy, embarrassment, guilt, and sadness.

It can take courage to acknowledge and express these types of emotions. It often feels easier and safer to hide behind anger and express outrage or indignation than to admit our real feelings. However, if we find the courage to acknowledge and discuss these underlying feelings, we can often let go of much of our anger.

In addition, those to whom we communicate openly are more likely to respond favorably to these honest statements about underlying feelings than to our anger and outrage. Honest expression of underlying feelings can thus short-circuit arguments and help move us and the other person toward finding solutions.

Here are some examples of honest expression of vulnerable feelings:

- I'm starting to realize that some of the irritation I've been feeling toward you is really because I've been envious of all the success you've been having, especially since I haven't felt as productive lately since my injury.

- I'm sorry for snapping. I'm not actually mad at you. I've just been feeling really worried and sad lately about my health decline.

- I think I've been blaming you so much because I didn't want to admit my own responsibility for what happened.

- When I heard someone repeat what I told you in confidence, I felt hurt and kind of betrayed.

- Sorry for being critical when you were talking about how impressed you are by your new coworker. I think I was just feeling a little jealous and insecure because I haven't been feeling as interesting or attractive since the accident.

Our willingness to self-disclose more vulnerable feelings will depend, of course, on the reasonable nature and kind spirit of the other person. There will always be some people whom we wisely choose not to confide in about vulnerable feelings.

Even in these cases, however, our own private recognition of our true feelings can help us stay calmer and think more reasonably about the best course of action. To process our feelings more fully later on, we might write about them in a journal or talk to a trusted friend about them.

Use the following worksheet to practice becoming aware of true feelings underlying angry reactions and how you might express these feelings to the other person.

■ Worksheet for Understanding and Expressing Feelings Underlying Anger

Observe your angry reactions over the next few days and describe below one or more episodes in which the anger seemed to serve as a shield to protect you against more vulnerable feelings, such as hurt, worry, jealousy, envy, embarrassment, guilt, or sadness.

What happened?

_____

_____

_____

_____

What was your underlying emotion?

_____

_____

_____

_____

What might you say to the other person to express your true feelings in order to bypass the need for protective anger?

_____

_____

_____

_____

How do you think that person would respond?

_____

_____

_____

_____

_____

Chapter 5   *Relationship Management*

The most important single ingredient in the formula of success is knowing how to get along with people.

              —Theodore Roosevelt

Social connections are vitally important to emotional well-being as well as to physical health. Scientific research has convincingly shown that strong social ties help us stay happier and healthier, keep our brains working better into old age, and even prolong our lives.

When physical or mental abilities decline as a result of injury, illness, pain, or just the normal effects of aging, social ties become even more important because of the greater need to rely on others for support and assistance.

However, just when social ties become more important as a result of changes in ability, they may also become harder to maintain. Partly, this is because the process of adjusting to changes in physical or mental abilities can be highly stressful, putting strain on important relationships.

Loss of abilities may also lead to loss of regular contact with friends from work or from recreational activities that can no longer be performed. Skill and effort are needed to keep some of these important social connections going and to form new friendships to take the place of those that are lost.

Sometimes, self-consciousness about visible signs of disability can lead to feelings of awkwardness and social anxiety, further adding to the challenge of maintaining old friendships and forming new ones.

For all these reasons, polishing your skills at developing and maintaining strong social connections can be helpful in adapting to a loss of ability. In this chapter, we'll review some of these skills. While you'll likely find that most of these skills are familiar to you already, they are offered here as reminders because the stress of major life change sometimes causes basic social skills to be put on the back burner, especially when interacting with family and close friends.

Increasing Cooperation

It can be difficult to adapt to needing more help. This difficulty stems in part from the blow to pride and self-image that can occur when we need more help. Chapter 2 of this book, Mood Regulation, addresses ways to manage this challenge to self-esteem caused by greater reliance on others.

In this section, we'll focus more on the challenge of how to ask for needed help, and to sustain this help over time, in ways that both we and our helpers can feel good about.

To start, let's review a few general observations about human nature:

- Most people feel a sense of satisfaction from being helpful.

- Most people feel upset when they see others in distress.

- Thus, most people are primed to want to help when they see that someone genuinely needs help.

- When helpers' efforts are acknowledged with expressions of gratitude, this validates that they've been helpful, makes them feel good about what they've done, and motivates them to help again.

- On the other hand, most people dislike being ordered to do things.

- Most people also dislike being taken advantage of, being taken for granted, or being criticized.

- Thus, if we issue demands or ask others to do things that we clearly can do for ourselves, we're likely to be resented.

- Likewise, if we fail to show appreciation or criticize how help was offered, we may discourage offers of further help.

Based on these general observations about human nature, here are some suggestions for how to promote helpfulness and cooperation.

First, think about whether you really need the help or could actually do the task yourself. If you can do the task safely and efficiently yourself, others may feel taken advantage of if you ask them to do it. This can contribute to resentment and caregiver burnout. Doing as much as you can for yourself also helps you stay stronger and more capable.

If you really do need help, then try to *ask rather than demand*. Because most people generally like to be helpful, they respond better when requests are phrased something like this:

- "Could you please _____?"

- "I'd really appreciate it if you'd _____."

- "Would you like to give me a hand with this _____?"

- "Could you do me a favor and _____?"

- "Do you think you'd be able to help me _____?"

- "It'd be a tremendous help if you could _____."

- "I wonder if you'd mind _____."

Phrasing your requests in this way allows your helpers to feel like they're actively choosing to be of assistance rather than being forced to do so. When people feel like they're choosing to be helpful, this activates their *altruism*, which is the natural tendency to enjoy being helpful to others.

Not only are you getting your needs met when you do this, you're also contributing to your helpers' happiness and sense of self-worth. And you're making it more likely that they'll want to help you in the future.

Asking rather than demanding is a good start, but most people also like to be sincerely thanked and complimented after they've done something helpful. Here are some examples of ways to thank and compliment:

- "Thanks. I really appreciate your help."

- "You're a lifesaver!"

- "I can't thank you enough."

- "I'm so grateful to have such a good friend."

- "Wow! You're really good at _____."

- "I couldn't have done it without you."

Such expressions of gratitude and compliments are usually received even better if delivered with a smile and good eye contact.

Some people feel a bit awkward and unsure about how to respond when they receive praise, but generally still appreciate having their efforts recognized. If your helper is uncomfortable with elaborate praise, just keep it simple and brief.

Not all helpers do things exactly the way you prefer. In fact, more often than not, they probably don't. If their shortcoming is fairly minor, it's often wise to lower your standards a bit. You may want to review Chapter 4, Anger and Frustration Management, to refresh your memory of ways to talk to yourself to decrease frustration.

If a helper's efforts to help you need to be fine-tuned, blunt criticism isn't usually the best strategy. It's generally more effective to first express thanks and point out what was done well. Then you can suggest a way the two of you might try something a bit different the next time. For example, you might try saying something like this:

> "Thanks. I appreciate your doing such a good job of helping me transfer from my wheelchair to the car. Next time let's see if we can make the transfer even safer by locking both brakes."

Following up the constructive feedback with another compliment can further contribute to the feedback being well received; this compliment–feedback–compliment approach is sometimes referred to as a "feedback sandwich."

Some of the techniques that work well for behavior management with children also happen to work well with adults. For example, giving positive attention for the behavior you like generally works better than criticizing the behavior you don't like. And when offering feedback, try for a ratio of about four positive comments for every constructive criticism. Naturally, if something is unsafe or otherwise just unacceptable, you can be more direct.

If you're paying well for service, you might not feel quite the same need to work at maintaining your caregiver's helpful attitude. Generally, though, even paid helpers function better over time when treated with respect and courtesy. Also, even though you may be paying generously for help through an agency or facility, the actual people who help you may not be so well paid.

Although helping others can be very rewarding, it can also be draining if the helper doesn't have a chance to take regular breaks. So, if possible, encourage helpers to take frequent breaks from their caregiving roles.

If your helper is also your spouse or significant other, the blending of these two roles can put considerable strain on your relationship. Bringing in outside caregivers can help to reduce that strain, if you have the resources to do so. If not, it's extra important to practice the relationship skills discussed in this chapter and to make sure you're doing as much as possible to reduce your dependency by taking care of your own needs.

On the following worksheet, write down names of people you want to practice these skills with and ways you'd like to phrase requests, thanks, compliments, and suggestions for change.

■ **Communication Skills for Increasing Cooperation Worksheet**

List the people with whom you want to practice these communication skills:

_____

_____

List some ways you'd like to ask for help:

_____

_____

_____

_____

List some ways you'd like to express gratitude:

_____

_____

_____

_____

List some ways you'd like to phrase compliments:

_____

_____

_____

_____

List some ways you'd like to suggest changes in how help is offered:

_____

_____

_____

_____

_____

As our abilities change, our social circles also often change. If we can no longer work, for example, our strong social connections with coworkers may start to weaken. The result is often similar when changes in ability prevent us from participating in the same social and recreational activities as before.

With effort and creativity, some close relationships may continue in a modified way. For example, we might arrange with our best friends from work to meet for lunch on an occasional basis even though we're no longer seeing each other regularly in the workplace. Or we might still attend our team's softball games even though we can no longer play.

Even with good planning, flexibility, and creativity, however, some important social connections may be lost or greatly weakened, leaving a void in our lives. To fill some of that social void with new people, it's often necessary to push ourselves to venture out to new settings:

- If abilities have changed as a result of injury or illness, we may find support groups available to provide opportunities to bond with others dealing with similar adjustments.

- If changing abilities are due simply to aging, senior centers and senior groups, available in most communities, can be a means of meeting new people.

- Most communities also have colleges or other places to take classes and meet new people at the same time.

- If we're unable to do the same work as before, a different job, paid or volunteer, will put us in contact with other potential new friends.

- We might join a social club, religious organization, political campaign, gym, yoga studio, or sports team or club.

Once in a social setting that provides opportunities to form new friendships, how is this done? Some people seem blessed with the "gift of gab" and ability to connect effortlessly with strangers. My wife, for example, is such a natural at striking up conversations with strangers that her father used to joke on family road trips that she seemed to be running for mayor of every rest stop, small town, and roadside attraction. Other people, myself included, don't find it so easy to connect with strangers. In fact, had I written this particular section of this chapter earlier in life, I might have felt compelled to include a disclaimer: "The author doesn't know what he's writing about."

It turns out, though, that there are specific, teachable skills my wife and others use to perform the social alchemy of turning strangers into acquaintances and, sometimes, friends. Over the years, I've managed to pick up a few of these skills for forming new connections with people. I'll describe some of what I've learned next, with assurance to you that my wife, the perpetual mayoral candidate, has read and approved of my message. If you share her natural gift for forming new social connections, feel free to jump ahead.

If you're still with me, let's think about some steps to follow in forming connections with others in new social settings. There's obviously no one set of steps that will work in every situation, but here's a rough guide for how new acquaintances can sometimes be made:

- Briefly make eye contact with others around you with a friendly expression on your face. If you're not quite sure how to look friendly, just smile slightly by turning up the corners of your mouth a bit. If you can crinkle the corners of your eyes a little to involve them in the smile, all the better, since this tends to make your friendly expression look more sincere. A fake "beauty pageant" smile doesn't seem to have the same effect as a sincere smile. If your forehead is tense, see if you can relax it a bit. A relaxed, happy expression tends to be more appealing to others.

- If your eye contact is returned and the person looks friendly, then smile a little more.

- If you see a smile in return, offer a brief greeting, such as "Hi" or "How's it going?"

- If the other person responds in a friendly way, then you might ask how he or she is enjoying whatever is going on in the social setting, or just comment on the weather.

- If the person responds and seems open to talking a bit more, you might then introduce yourself.

- When your new acquaintance shares his or her name, use the techniques described in Chapter 6, Memory Management, to try to remember it.

- You might then ask a few questions about the person's background, experiences, and interests.

- If the person seems to enjoy talking about him- or herself, and most people do, keep up the conversation until you find something in common. What you share might be an acquaintance, a hobby, a geographical connection, or a cause you both support.

- If the person shows interest in continuing the conversation or planning some joint activities, you may be on your way to a new friendship. You might at this point exchange contact information.

But don't take it personally or be overly disappointed if the conversation winds down without a great mutual desire for further contact, as is usually the case. At least you've made an acquaintance, and maybe that acquaintance will become a friend over time or introduce you to someone else with whom you have more in common. It normally takes many such encounters before a true and lasting friendship is formed. Fortunately, a small number of close friendships is all most of us need and have time to maintain.

Whether connecting with new people or reconnecting with people you already know, it's common to feel some self-consciousness about a new disability that's outwardly visible to others. Some people react by avoiding going out in public, but avoidance is not an adaptive way to deal with this social discomfort.

You'll generally be better off pushing yourself to be socially active, recognizing that self-consciousness typically decreases gradually as you spend more time out in public. For more discussion of this topic, you may want to refer back to the "Avoid Avoidance" section in Chapter 3, Stress and Anxiety Management.

In addition to the self-consciousness you may feel as you adapt to being a person with a visible disability, there may also be some initial awkwardness felt by new people you meet, or even old friends who knew you before your disability. They may, for example, be curious about your disability, but unsure of whether they should ask about it.

They may also have some misconceptions. For example, they might assume that use of a wheelchair means that you also have mental limitations or assume that your disability makes you miserable and deserving of pity. Or they might place you on a pedestal, assuming that you must be a "hero" or unusually well-adjusted to be able to deal with a disability or that you must have some special abilities in other areas. (If you're interested in learning more about some of these social dynamics, they are well described in an interesting book by psychologist Dr. Dana Dunn: *The Social Psychology of Disability*.)

Generally, awkwardness and misconceptions of this type become less and less of an issue as you and the other person interact on a human-to-human level. Again, the solution is engagement, not avoidance.

Use the following worksheet to plan how you'll increase your social connections.

■ Social Connection Planning Worksheet

List one or more friends you'd like to stay in contact with even though you're no longer seeing each other as regularly because of a change in your social circles:

_____

_____

_____

_____

_____

Describe a plan for maintaining regular contact with that friend or those friends:

_____

_____

_____

_____

_____

Pick one or more of the social settings below that you're willing to try as a way to meet new people and then write down your plan for doing this.

■ Support group: _____

■ Senior center or senior group: _____

■ College or other educational setting: _____

■ Volunteer or paid work: _____

■ Social club: _____

■ Religious organization: _____

■ Political campaign: _____

■ Gym or yoga studio: _____

■ Sports team or club: _____

■ Other: _____

Your ability to develop and maintain successful relationships depends in part on how well you show others that they're liked, listened to, and appreciated. In this section, we'll review a few skills that help to communicate the positive regard you have for the important people in your life.

Have you ever wondered why dogs are so beloved by so many people? It probably has a lot to do with the way dogs react to their human companions. Dogs run to the door, wag their tails, and sometimes jump and squeal with delight when we come home, even if we've only stepped out to check the mail. Our human companions, by contrast, may not even look up from whatever they're doing.

Most of us are "hardwired" to like being liked, and dogs are masters of showing how much they like us. This skill that dogs naturally possess can be developed to make important people in our lives feel more liked and valued.

Squealing and wagging are most likely not your style, but a warm, happy smile and greeting will usually be enough to show that you care. Asking how their day has gone, and listening to their response, also shows interest and concern.

The importance of listening is difficult to overstate. You can show you're listening closely by making eye contact and nodding, smiling, or expressing other reactions, as appropriate, to what's being said.

Letting others talk without much interruption is also generally a good idea. If there's a pause, you can show interest by asking questions for clarification or inquiring about additional details. If they say something funny, make sure you smile or laugh.

When people tell you about problems they're having, it's wise to hesitate before offering advice unless you've been specifically asked to give advice. Often people just want acknowledgment of their feelings about the difficult situation they're going through.

After you've offered this acknowledgment and support, you may still have some helpful advice you'd like to offer. Before offering your advice, however, consider asking if advice is actually wanted. For example, you might say something like this:

> "That sounds like a difficult situation. It must be really frustrating and hard to deal with. How do you think you're going to handle it?"

If they sound like they've thought it through well and have a reasonable solution, you might choose to withhold your suggestions and just say something supportive like this:

> "Sounds like a good plan."

If, on the other hand, they don't have a plan, or their plan seems very questionable, you might say something like this:

> "That seems like it's going to be a real challenge. Let me know if there's anything I can do or if you just want me to help you brainstorm some ways of dealing with it."

Here are some other ways to show that you like and care about others:

- Remembering what they've told you

- Remembering and thanking them for their gifts, favors, and other acts of kindness

- Remembering to keep secret what they've told you in confidence

- Remembering and asking about their interests and hobbies

- Remembering and taking into account their tastes and preferences

- Remembering and acknowledging important events in their lives, such as birthdays

- Remembering and commenting on the successes of their favorite sports teams

If you're not good at remembering this type of information, learn and apply some of the strategies in Chapter 6, Memory Management.

For many people, a powerful way to show that you care is to express genuine interest and concern for the welfare and accomplishments of their family members, both the human ones and the four-legged ones.

Do all these things to help others feel liked and appreciated, and most often they'll like and appreciate you in return. Even if you don't quite rise to the level of importance of their pets, you'll usually become more closely bonded as a result of these efforts. And, over time, the initial feeling that it's an effort to do these behaviors will lessen as relationships strengthen and provide more and more enjoyment.

When our abilities are diminished, we may fear others will not like us as much because we have less to offer in terms of knowledge or skill. It helps to recall another Theodore Roosevelt quote that conveys much wisdom about human nature:

> Nobody cares how much you know, until they know how much you care.

The point is that our efforts to show our knowledge and skills might be better spent showing how much we care about others in our lives. The better we do this, the less our friends and family will care that we can no longer do everything we could do before.

Chapter 6

Memory Management

While no one has a perfect memory, forgetfulness is more common in those whose brains have been affected by injury, illness, pain, advancing age, or emotional distress.

When this happens, we tend not to lose our memories from earlier in life. What usually declines most is the capacity to form and recall new memories. Here are some examples of this kind of memory difficulty:

- Being unable to recall where we've placed our keys or important documents or where we've parked our car

- Forgetting why we've walked into a room or what we intended to buy when shopping

- Forgetting the names of people we've just met or what we've recently read or seen on television

- Having trouble learning to use new technology or remembering directions to new locations

- Forgetting to follow through on something we intended to do

Sometimes information is not actually forgotten, but is hard to access when we need it. For example, we might struggle to find a word to express ourselves in conversation or have trouble recalling the name of an old friend or famous movie actor even though we know that we still know it.

Such experiences can be frustrating, especially when we compare our current memory performance to earlier times in life when memory seemed to work almost effortlessly. Fortunately, though, better day-to-day memory functioning is possible for those willing to practice the techniques described in this chapter. For example, in this first section, you'll learn ways to make sure you don't miss appointments or fail to follow through on things you've agreed to do.

We've all had the experience of forgetting about some event, appointment, or obligation, perhaps an assignment for school or work, a bill payment, or the birthday of a loved one. The embarrassment, hurt feelings, late penalties, and other consequences of such forgetfulness can usually be avoided by using the following techniques:

◾ Purchase an appointment book or daily planner, preferably one small enough that you can carry it with you almost everywhere, but large enough to write in comfortably. (It's helpful if it also contains a section for addresses and phone numbers.) Use your appointment book or planner as follows:

1. Record all appointments, plans, anniversaries, birthdays, and obligations on the appropriate dates.

2. Never agree to go anywhere or do anything in the future without immediately writing that plan down on the date or dates that you will need to take action on it.

3. Review your appointment book or planner every morning and again several times throughout the day.

4. Also review your appointment book or planner each night to see what your plans are for the next day and for the rest of the week.

5. As you accomplish each task, cross it off with a single line so you can still read it to see what you've done.

6. If you don't accomplish a task on the day you intended, cross it off your schedule on that date and transfer it to the next reasonable date that you can accomplish it.

7. Draw an arrow after each entry that is a recurring meeting or responsibility. For example, if you have a meeting the first Wednesday of each month, draw an arrow after that entry (e.g., "Bridge Club 2:00 p.m. first Wednesday of each

month →"). As you cross that entry off after the meeting, you'll notice the arrow and be reminded to mark that event down on your schedule for the next month.

- For tasks that need to be done at a specific time, alarm clocks or timers can be useful. Most basic cell phones and all smartphones and tablet computers have this alarm or reminder capability. Wrist watches with built-in alarms are convenient since you can easily take them with you wherever you go. If you need assistance setting up such devices to alert you at the right time, just ask a friend or relative who's good with technology to help.

- Another technique to jog your memory about things you need to do is to put notes or other reminders where you're likely to see them (e.g., on the bathroom mirror, by the front door, attached to your key ring, on the refrigerator). Self-sticking note pads are especially handy for this purpose. Just be careful to take your notes down when the task is finished, and don't use so many that you start to ignore them.

- To make sure you don't forget to pay bills, it's best to pay them as soon as you open them, before you even set them down. If you need to wait until you have the money to pay your bills, write a note in your appointment book or planner for the date when you will be able to pay them. Then make sure you store your bills in a special place where you'll always know to find them, preferably right next to your checkbook and stamps. If you regularly have enough money in your account to cover your bills, consider setting them up to be automatically paid by your bank. Your credit card, mortgage, insurance, and utility companies will often help you set up automatic payments.

- For the kind of forgetting that happens in the middle of a task, such as walking into a room and not remembering why you went there, try one or both of these techniques:

    1. Repeat your intention over and over in your mind until your mission is complete (e.g., "going to get the vacuum").

2. Picture yourself using the object you're going to get in some strange or comical way to make the memory stronger (e.g., vacuuming up all the furniture in the room).

■ For problems remembering steps in a routine, write the routine in the form of a numbered checklist and post it right where that activity normally takes place. As you perform each step, check it off. You can create checklists for complex, multi-step work responsibilities, as well as for simpler tasks, such as making sure you take everything you need with you when you leave home.

Complete the following worksheet to help you learn the techniques you just read about and plan how to apply them in your daily life.

▨ Remembering Future Events, Appointments, and Obligations Worksheet

Put in your own words how you could use an appointment book or daily planner to help you keep track of future events, appointments, and obligations:

_____

_____

Put in your own words how you could use alarms or timers to help you keep track of future events, appointments, and obligations:

_____

_____

Put in your own words how you could use self-sticking notes or other physical reminders to help you keep track of future events, appointments, and obligations:

_____

_____

Put in your own words how you could handle the problem of forgetting what your intention was, such as why you walked into another room:

_____

_____

Put in your own words how you could use a checklist to help you remember a multi-step routine:

_____

_____

Now pick at least one of the memory techniques you just wrote about and state your specific plans for trying it out over the next few days:

_____

_____

_____

_____

One of the most common memory complaints is inability to remember the names of new acquaintances. The techniques described next can help you become better at this useful social skill:

One very important principle of memory is that *the more we think about new information, the better it sticks*. While this principle seems like common sense, many of us ignore it when we're introduced to someone new. We hear the new name but immediately shift our attention to what we want to say. By doing so, we make it much less likely that we'll remember the name. So take a moment when you meet someone new to think about his or her name, and perhaps to comment on it. Here are some examples of ways to get yourself thinking about a name so that you're more likely to remember it:

1. You might note whether the first or last name is the same as that of a friend or of someone famous. If it's a last name that they share, perhaps you can inquire about whether they're related.

2. If the name is unusual, you might ask how it's spelled or inquire about its national origin.

3. Many last names originally had some meaning that you can think about as a way to get your brain to more actively process the new information. For example, you might wonder if Mrs. Goldsmith had an ancestor who made things out of gold or if Mr. Wilson had an ancestor who was the son of someone named "Will."

4. You might think to yourself of a humorous or otherwise memorable association between the person's name and his or her job or appearance. For example, if your new plumber happens to be named "John," you might remind yourself that some people use this name as another term for "toilet." Or you might make a mental note that your new acquaintance "Paul" is unusually pale.

5. Mental images make memories even stronger. In the plumber example above, if you picture the plumber's torso as a toilet, with his head, arms, and legs attached to it, you're more likely to remember his name is "John." The name "Mary" might stick better if you picture her standing at the altar in a wedding dress, and the name "Ralph" might stick better if you picture him "ralphing" (vomiting). To remember my last name, "Wanlass," you might picture me as a wizard who has lost his wand and is "wandless."

6. Rhymes also make names more memorable. My nickname "Rick," for example, has several easy rhymes. Some of these rhymes happen to be unflattering, but I don't need to know how you remember my name; I'll just be impressed that you do. Any technique that makes you actively think about new information, such as a name, will help you recall it later.

- A second important principle of memory is that *the more we use new information, the better we'll retain it in the future.* You can apply this principle when meeting someone new by using that person's name immediately (e.g., "Nice to meet you, Juanita") and again when the conversation ends (e.g., "Hope to see you again, Juanita"). If you can also work the name into the middle of the conversation, all the better.

- A third important principle of memory is that *reviewing or rehearsing information periodically over time helps you to retain it.* You can apply this principle when you've met someone new by thinking about that person's name several times later in the day and over the next few days. If you're not sure you'll remember the name long enough to review it later, ask for a business card or write down the person's name and a few identifying characteristics as soon as possible. When you rehearse the person's name, try to also rehearse the mental images or other associations you used to try to remember it.

- Keeping such information in an address book will make it easier to find later. To be really thorough, you can enter it in your address book twice, once alphabetically and once under the name of the place where you're likely to see that person again. For instance, you might list the key people you want to remember from a certain office or business under the name of that office or business in your address book. Then, right before you visit that place again, review the names and any important facts you've written about each person. This minute or so of extra review will pay off in better memory performance.

Complete the following worksheet to help you learn the techniques you just read about and plan how to apply them in your daily life.

▓ Remembering Names When Meeting People Worksheet

Put in your own words the three important general memory principles discussed in the previous section:

_____

_____

_____

_____

_____

Put in your own words the specific techniques you can use to remember names when you meet new people:

_____

_____

_____

_____

_____

Over the next few days, try out some of these techniques for learning the names of new acquaintances. Or you can practice these techniques as you watch news shows or talk shows on TV. Write about how you learned two new names using these techniques:

_____

_____

_____

_____

_____

_____

_____

Memory for what you read can be improved through the use of the *SQ3R* method, developed by psychology professor Dr. Francis Robinson. This method has five steps:

1. **S**: In the first step, you *survey* or *skim* the material, with special attention to chapter and section headings and any chapter summaries, to gain a general overview of what topics are covered and how they're organized.

2. **Q**: In the second step, you think of the specific *questions* that you hope to have answered through careful reading of the material. This helps you feel like you're reading for a purpose, which keeps you more focused and therefore more likely to remember what you read.

3. **R**: After this initial survey and formulation of questions, the third step is to actually *read* the material, searching for the answers to these questions.

4. **R**: The fourth step is to *recite* or *rehearse* in your own words the major points and important details of what you've read. It also helps to write a few notes about these major points and important details.

5. **R**: The fifth and final step is to *review* the material one last time to remind yourself of its major points, as well as how the specific details you've read relate to those major points.

This approach does take a bit more up-front time and effort, but research over the past few decades has shown that it improves ability to recall what you read.

Reading in a place with few distractions also helps. It's also a good idea to do your reading and other mentally demanding tasks in the morning or at whatever time of day you feel most alert.

Complete the following worksheet to help you learn the techniques you just read about and plan how to apply them in your daily life.

Remembering What You Read Worksheet

Put in your own words what needs to be done in each of the SQ3R steps.

■ **Survey:**

_____

_____

■ **Question:**

_____

_____

■ **Read:**

_____

_____

■ **Recite:**

_____

_____

■ **Review:**

_____

_____

Now apply the SQ3R method as you read something (e.g., the next page) and come back here and describe what you did and how well you were able to understand and remember what you read:

_____

_____

_____

_____

_____

_____

Have you ever lost your keys, misplaced a check, or forgotten where you parked your car? Everyone occasionally misplaces important belongings, but if this happens to you frequently, here are some solutions:

▪ You're less likely to lose track of your possessions if you follow this rule: *A place for everything and everything in its place.* So, take the time to decide where you'll routinely store your keys, phone, checkbook, shoes, and any other objects that are inconvenient to lose. Establish a filing system for important paperwork.

▪ As you assign each item a "home," write the name of the item and its home on a list. Then rewrite the list using some method of organization, such as alphabetical order or groupings of similar items. Leave space between items so you can easily add additional items as you think of them. Post your master list of object locations on a wall or refrigerator so you can't misplace it.

▪ Then make certain that you always return your belongings to their designated homes as soon as you're finished with them.

▪ Use your appointment book or planner to jot down the location of objects that you temporarily need to place away from their customary home. For example, when leaving your car in a parking garage, make a note of its location. Or use your smartphone to take a picture of the sign showing its location or to make a voice recording of its location. (Just don't let your smartphone battery run out.)

Complete the following worksheet to help you learn the techniques you just read about and plan how to apply them in your daily life.

■ Remembering Where You Place Belongings Worksheet

What does "A place for everything and everything in its place" mean, and do you think this would be a helpful rule for you to try to follow?

_____

_____

_____

_____

_____

_____

Think of two or three belongings you tend to misplace. Write them here along with the specific "homes" that you are assigning them to (e.g., My shoes will always be on my feet or in my closet, and my car keys will always be hanging by the front door, in my pocket, or in my ignition):

_____

_____

_____

_____

_____

_____

Put in your own words a technique you'll use to keep track of belongings that are temporarily out of their normal "home" (e.g., When I loan a tool to a neighbor, I'll write myself a note in my appointment book for the date we agree it will be returned):

_____

_____

_____

_____

_____

_____

Memory problems can be particularly dangerous when they result in the overuse or underuse of medications. Medications obviously don't work when they aren't taken, and overdoses can be toxic.

Both types of problems can result in unnecessary emergency room visits, hospitalizations, and deaths. Researchers have estimated costs in the hundreds of billions of dollars per year in the United States from failure to take medications as prescribed.

To reduce this risk, try these techniques:

- Buy a plastic medication dispenser with separate compartments for each day of the week. These inexpensive items are available in most drugstores and are helpful for keeping track of how many pills you've taken.

- If you take pills more than once a day, you might even buy more than one dispenser and clearly label each (e.g., "Morning Pills").

- Keep your medication dispenser in a place where you'll see it frequently, but out of reach of children and pets.

- Fill up your medication dispenser at the beginning of each week, placing the appropriate pills in each compartment.

- Set your cell phone, smartphone, or watch alarm to alert you each time you're due for another dose of medication.

- Use your appointment book or planner to write reminders to take your medications, fill up your pill dispenser, and refill prescriptions.

- Sign up for automatic prescription delivery if you're eligible for this service.

- Ask a trusted family member or friend to help you manage your medications.

Complete the following worksheet to help you learn the techniques you just read about and plan how to apply them in your daily life.

▪ Remembering to Take Medications Worksheet

Put in your own words what the specific dangers are for you if you forget to take your prescribed medications:

_____

_____

_____

_____

_____

Put in your own words what the specific dangers are for you if you forget that you've taken your prescribed medications already and end up taking too much:

_____

_____

_____

_____

_____

Now pick the memory techniques that you think will best help you keep track of your medications. Write down your specific plans for using these techniques over the next few weeks:

_____

_____

_____

_____

_____

_____

_____

_____

How often have you heard a joke, planned to tell it to a friend, and then just couldn't remember it? Some people are naturally gifted at remembering jokes, but most of us have to put in some extra effort. These techniques will help:

- Next time you hear a joke worth retelling, take out your appointment book or planner and write down the punch line and two or three key phrases.

- Rehearse the joke in your head until you have it right.

- Then actually tell that joke the same day to three or more different people. That will usually be enough to make a joke stick in your memory, at least for a while (unless of course it was a truly forgettable joke to begin with—you'll know that from the groans and rolled eyes of your audience).

The same method works when trying to remember an interesting fact or new vocabulary word:

- Write it down in your appointment book or planner.

- Rehearse it a few times in your head.

- Bring it up in conversation several times that day.

- Review the new fact or word again before going to bed that night.

Then, to make your new joke, fact, or word really stick with you, write it down in your appointment book or planner a few more times, spaced out in increasingly long intervals (e.g., 2 days, 4 days, 1 week, 2 weeks, 1 month, 2 months, 4 months).

Each time you see it in your appointment book or planner, bring up the new joke, fact, or word in conversation, or at least talk about it to yourself.

Periodically recalling and actively thinking about something over increasingly long intervals is one of the most important keys to forming durable memories.

Complete the following worksheet to help you learn the techniques you just read about and plan how to apply them in your daily life.

Put in your own words what was just described as one of the most important keys to forming durable memories:

_____

_____

_____

_____

_____

_____

Put in your own words the steps you can take to better learn new jokes, facts, and words:

_____

_____

_____

_____

_____

_____

Use these techniques to learn one or more new jokes, facts, or words and come back and write about how you did it here:

_____

_____

_____

_____

_____

_____

_____

_____

_____

If you have trouble remembering what you've done or talked about, it helps to make a summary of each important event or discussion.

When talking with someone, you can do this by summarizing out loud what you heard the other person say and asking him or her if you understood correctly. This technique not only helps you remember the conversation, but also helps you avoid miscommunication and shows the other person that you care about what he or she has to say.

Immediately after each important event or conversation, make a record of what happened. This record can be in the form of brief notes entered into your appointment book or planner. If you run out of room, you can use a separate notepad. Or you can dictate notes to yourself with your smartphone or voice recorder.

Make a record of the people you talked to, what you talked about, how you felt, and what you did each day. The process of writing or talking about your experiences helps you to remember them. Reviewing at the end of the day what you've written or recorded further helps you remember.

To make your memories even stronger and more durable, keep a separate journal or diary at home (so you never lose it) and write a summary of the day's events before you go to sleep. Following is a form that can be copied and used for recording and reinforcing your important memories each day. If you prefer, you can purchase a journal, diary, or full-size day planner to use for this purpose.

As you put the day's events and conversations into words again, the memory traces will grow stronger, and during sleep they may continue to strengthen. And if you still forget some of the details, you'll at least have a written record to remind you.

Memory Reinforcement Log

Date: _____

Past: Events or information from yesterday or the recent past that I don't want to forget:

_____

_____

_____

Present: Events or information from today that I don't want to forget:

_____

_____

_____

Highlights of my day (e.g., what I enjoyed, what I feel grateful for, how I showed kindness to others):

_____

_____

_____

_____

_____

Future: Plans for tomorrow and the near future that I don't want to forget:

_____

_____

_____

Steps I have taken so I won't forget to carry out these plans:

_____

_____

_____

Some of us are bothered by a mixture of forgetfulness and anxiety that shows up in nagging doubts, such as not being sure if we've locked the door, closed the garage, set the alarm, turned off the stove, or shut the gate. These nagging doubts generally apply to actions performed on autopilot, without thinking much about them.

Memory traces are less strong for actions done on autopilot, so a solution to this type of memory problem is to perform these tasks in a more mindful, aware state. You might, for example, say out loud, "Locking the door at 7:34 on Monday morning."

If you need even more reassurance, you can write a brief note in your appointment book or planner (e.g., Locked door 7:34).

Complete the following worksheet to help you learn the techniques you just read about and plan how to apply them in your daily life.

Put in your own words a technique you can use in conversation to make sure you understand and remember what the other person said:

_____

_____

_____

_____

_____

Put in your own words some other techniques for remembering important things you've talked about and done:

_____

_____

_____

_____

_____

_____

Make some copies of the Memory Reinforcement Log in this section and fill out one for each of the next three nights. Then come back and write here about whether you found this technique helpful:

_____

_____

_____

_____

_____

_____

_____

Some people are great with directions and seem to almost have built-in compasses. Most of us, though, have to try a little harder and rely more on written notes, maps, or modern technology.

GPS technology has made it much easier to navigate to places you want to go, even if your memory for directions is poor. If you have a smartphone or GPS navigation device, enter the locations you want to be able to find and set them as "favorites." (To prevent accidents, never enter information into your smartphone or GPS device while driving.) Or if your smartphone or GPS device has voice recognition ability, just tell it where you want to go. If necessary, ask a friend or relative who's good with gadgets to train you to use GPS technology.

If you don't have a GPS device or smartphone, or if you're in a location where GPS signals are weak, then you can rely on your address book. List the addresses of places you need to go and write out directions in as much detail as you will need. Help with getting turn-by-turn directions is readily available on the Internet on sites such as *Google Maps* and *MapQuest*.

Complete the following worksheet to help you learn the techniques you just read about and plan how to apply them in your daily life.

■ Remembering Addresses and Directions Worksheet

Put in your own words some ways you can keep track of addresses and directions without electronic devices:

_____

_____

_____

_____

Put in your own words some ways you can keep track of addresses and directions using electronic devices:

_____

_____

_____

_____

Describe a recent situation in which you were lost or were unsure of how to get to where you wanted to go:

_____

_____

_____

_____

State the specific steps you'll take to make sure that you don't have this same problem again:

_____

_____

_____

_____

_____

The simplest way to deal with forgetfulness when shopping is to write down what you need in your appointment book or planner. Or use a separate piece of paper if your list is lengthy. Then just cross off each item as you find it at the store. The same method can be used for to-do lists. You can also find free smartphone apps for shopping and to-do lists.

There are more advanced techniques for quickly committing lists to memory without relying on notes. You can find these described in books on memory at your local library or on websites such as http://www.wikihow.com. While these techniques can be used very effectively, most people won't put forth the effort to learn and implement them. It's simply much easier to write a list.

If, however, you want to master one of these advanced memory techniques, here's a brief description of one that works quite well.

The Roman Room Memory Technique

Think of the house or apartment you've lived in for the longest time or know best. Draw a rough floor plan. Identify ten different rooms or locations (front porch, entry hall, etc.) on your drawing and number them in the order you would see them as you walked through. Give them each both a number and a descriptive label (e.g., kitchen or back patio).

Then draw the floor plan with numbers and descriptive labels again, trying not to look at your first drawing. Now make sure that the drawings match.

Once you have a consistent map of numbered locations on paper, close your eyes and imagine going through each location in order, each time saying the number and name of the location. Practice this many times over several days until you can easily see the map in your imagination.

When you have this map of ten locations firmly stored in memory, you're ready to begin using it to remember other information. Here's what you do:

- Have someone give you a list of three things, such as grocery items, to remember.

- Picture the first item in location 1, but make your mental picture extra memorable by seeing the item as really big, funny, or active in some way. If the first item is sugar, for example, and the first location is your driveway, you might picture a mountain of sugar in your driveway, perhaps with you skiing down it or a giant colony of ants eating it.

- Do the same thing for the other two items on the list, placing them in the next two locations on your mental map.

- Then see if you can remember all three items.

- Once you master a list of three items, add one more and gradually work your way up to ten.

- Test yourself on trips to the grocery store (but keep a backup list in your pocket or purse just in case you need it). The more you practice, the more easily you'll be able to quickly make memorable mental images and assign them to locations. As you gain more skill and confidence, you'll find that the backup list is no longer always necessary.

- Once you can handle ten items, consider adding a few more locations to your mental map so you can remember longer lists.

This technique works best for information you only need to remember for a while, because as you learn new lists, the new memories of objects in those locations will crowd out the old ones.

However, if you need to hold onto important information over time, you can create an additional mental map of another familiar location to store that information on a long-term basis.

Complete the following worksheet to help you learn the techniques you just read about and plan how to apply them in your daily life.

Remembering Shopping Lists and To-Do Lists Worksheet

Describe in your own words the simplest way of making sure you don't forget items on shopping lists and to-do lists:

_____

_____

Describe in your own words the steps involved in learning and using the Roman Room Memory Technique:

_____

_____

_____

_____

_____

_____

Draw a familiar floor plan and number ten locations on it below:

Now have someone tell you a list of at least three items and see if you can use the Roman Room Memory Technique to remember them. Describe how this technique worked for you:

_____

_____

_____

_____

Now that you've read through these techniques once, your work has really just begun. Many people read this kind of self-improvement information, tell themselves it sounds helpful, and then put the material away and never change a thing. For these techniques to actually work, you have to work at them.

See if you can find a partner to help make practicing these techniques more fun. Almost everyone wishes his or her memory could be better, so finding a partner or several partners to work with shouldn't be too difficult. By helping to teach these techniques to others, you'll increase your own expertise.

It's usually best to work on mastering just one technique at a time. Any change in how you do things is likely to be a challenge, so give yourself plenty of time to work on each technique. Write notes or set alarms to remind yourself to practice.

If a technique doesn't work quite right for you, think creatively about how you can fine-tune it so it does work for you. Then, as you master one technique, move on to another.

Once you've mastered most of these techniques and begun to use them on a daily basis, you'll make fewer memory errors. You might even notice that your stress level decreases as you discover that you can count on yourself to function more reliably. Memory tends to work better when chronic stress is kept in check, so using these memory techniques may help protect your brain's memory ability.

Other stress management techniques, such as meditation, may also help with memory. Review Chapter 3, Stress and Anxiety Management, if you want to refresh your memory of some of these techniques.

Keeping stress in check is just one way to maintain your brain's memory systems. Other important protective steps include staying socially and physically active, taking medications as prescribed and going for regular medical checkups, and keeping a positive outlook.

If you want your memory and other mental abilities to stay strong, be careful about what you put into your body. For example, smoking tobacco decreases oxygen supply to the brain and significantly increases the risk of dementia. Marijuana use is known to impair memory, as is excessive alcohol consumption.

People who eat "brain-healthy" foods have a substantially reduced risk of developing dementia. For example, support has been found for the MIND diet, which emphasizes healthy foods such as leafy green vegetables, berries (especially blueberries), whole grains, nuts, beans, and olive oil.

Adequate sleep is also important, since some memories formed earlier in the day appear to be strengthened during sleep.

If you've been told that you snore loudly, make gasping sounds, or stop breathing at times during sleep, ask your healthcare providers to make sure you don't have obstructive sleep apnea, as this condition can impair your memory and cause other health problems.

When memory errors do happen, don't waste energy being overly upset with yourself. Instead, think of each memory failure as a learning opportunity. Focus on figuring out where your memory technique broke down and how you can modify your technique to work more reliably next time. Or be creative and invent a new memory technique that will prevent that problem from occurring again.

It's not by chance that this pain management chapter is the last chapter in the book. Rather, it's by design, because chronic pain management requires all of the skills taught in the previous chapters.

To live well with chronic pain, you must be skilled at maintaining a positive mood, motivating yourself, regulating your stress level, and getting along with others. Pain and pain medications can make it harder to focus and, therefore, harder to remember, so you also need to know how to stay on top of things mentally. In this chapter we'll put together the skills learned in the previous chapters, along with some new skills, to help you formulate a plan for living a good life despite chronic pain.

Injuries and illnesses are frequently accompanied by pain. Even without a specific injury or illness, the aging body experiences gradual deterioration of joints and other body parts, often leading to pain.

Sometimes pain associated with injury, illness, or aging resolves in a short time, but sometimes it lasts for months or years. Pain that persists for a few months or longer is considered *chronic pain*, and this type of pain poses a special challenge to coping resources.

Painful conditions should, of course, be brought to the attention of healthcare providers and reasonable attempts made to find treatments that help to correct the underlying problem and relieve the pain.

Unfortunately, despite tremendous advances in some areas of healthcare, well over a billion people worldwide are estimated to suffer from chronic pain. In fact, in the United States, chronic pain affects more people than heart disease, cancer, and diabetes combined.

It's normal to feel frustrated and perhaps even desperate when told that there's nothing more that can be done to get rid of the pain. Among the unpopular messages delivered by healthcare providers, "You'll have to live with it" probably ranks as only slightly less upsetting than "You may want to get your affairs in order" and "I'm going to need the names and addresses of all your current and former partners." However, if you've been told that your pain condition can't be completely fixed by healthcare providers or totally controlled by medications, then it makes sense to learn to better manage the pain yourself.

To start, it helps to have a basic understanding of where pain signals come from and how the brain processes them. Most pain arises from irritation to pain nerves in your body. These pain nerves send a signal through the spinal cord and then to the brain, where the signal is recognized and interpreted as pain. The same amount of injury or irritation to the pain nerves, however, does not always result in the same amount of pain. Sometimes, for example, a minor injury is felt as more painful than a major one.

In trying to understand how this could be, pain scientists have developed the concept of a "pain gate." This can be thought of as a mechanism whereby the nervous system is able to regulate the amount of pain signal it receives and processes.

As shown in Figure 7.1, some factors push the pain gate more open, which allows greater signal through to be processed by the brain as pain. And other factors push the pain gate more shut, allowing less pain signal through.

For example, stress, depressed mood, and anger often result in opening of the pain gate, which worsens pain suffering. By contrast, relaxing or focusing on an enjoyable activity results in closing of the pain gate and thus less perception of pain. Most people who have chronic pain can readily understand this pain gate concept when it's explained to them and can relate it to their own variations in pain experience.

It isn't realistic to think of totally shutting the pain gate; it's just important to recognize that you have some influence over how open it is. Adopting this perspective allows you to avoid two potential traps:

- One trap is excessive, passive *dependency* on others, such as healthcare providers, to take away your pain when in fact they've already done their best to provide relief.

152

How the Pain Gate Works

Positive Emotions   Forgiveness/Acceptance

　　　　　Stress Reduction
　　　　　　　　　　　Pleasant Activities
Sleep/Rest

　　　　　　　　Meditation
Movement/Exercise
　　　　　　　　　　　Muscle Relaxation

Sense of Control   Relaxed Breathing

Overactivity   Tension   Anger

　　　　　　　　　Depression
Inactivity   Exhaustion

　　　　　　　Helplessness
Stress
　　　　　　　　　Pain Focus

Figure 7.1

Pain gate and how it works.

The other trap is *helplessness*, a psychological state that itself can push the pain gate more open. Thinking about your pain with the pain gate in mind helps you to feel responsible for and capable of taking active steps to manage your pain and suffering.

So, one of the first important shifts in thinking about chronic pain is recognizing that you can take an active role in dealing with it and are not totally dependent on others to "fix" you.

Another important shift is to realize that the steps you take to manage pain will each be only partial solutions. With some healthcare problems, such as appendicitis, the solution can be a single fix, such as appendectomy. Chronic pain, by contrast, generally requires multiple solutions, and it requires that these solutions be applied over and over on a daily basis.

In this way, chronic pain is more like some other chronic health conditions that require active, daily management. Think of a person with heart disease or diabetes, for example, who has to incorporate lifestyle changes such as healthier nutrition, increased exercise, and stress reduction.

With chronic pain, there are multiple partial solutions that can help, but many people don't use them consistently because they're stuck on the idea of a single solution applied one time. Those who deal well with chronic pain apply multiple solutions, each of which might only help a small amount (say, 5% or 10%) but together add up to significant help. And they employ these solutions on an ongoing basis.

In the sections that follow, we'll review twelve of these pain management solutions, starting with the skill of pacing yourself so you can still be productive despite pain. Our goal will be to help you identify potentially useful new pain management strategies you might want to try, as well as to recognize and refine strategies that you may already be using.

Activity Pacing

Many people with chronic pain alternate between overactivity and underactivity. When they have a "good day," with a little break from the normal intensity of their pain, they try to catch up on tasks they've been postponing because of pain.

Typically, they overdo, experience a pain flare-up and fatigue, and set themselves back so that they're even less productive than usual over the following few days. For example, they might spend several hours on a "good day" planting a spring garden and then be too sore and tired to tend the garden or follow through on other commitments during the "bad days" that follow.

To avoid these flare-ups and prolonged "down times," it's smart to *pace* yourself so that you do a reasonable amount of productive activity each day, with your own good judgment determining how much you do, rather than your pain being in charge. This steady, consistent approach generally allows you to be more productive overall and to be more able to follow through on plans you make with others.

Thinking about pacing also encourages you to break big tasks that seem overwhelming and never seem to get done into smaller ones that you're more likely to actually begin to tackle. For a refresher on how to break bigger tasks into smaller ones and keep yourself motivated, feel free to go back and review Chapter 1, Self-Management: Changing Behavior and Thoughts.

Use the following worksheet to better understand the concept of pacing and to make some plans for using this strategy more regularly.

▪ Activity Pacing Worksheet

Think about a time in the last few months when you didn't pay enough attention to pacing yourself and ended up overdoing an activity to the point of having a setback. Describe what happened:

_____

_____

_____

_____

Think about how you could handle a similar situation in the future by making a greater effort to pace yourself. Describe what you would do:

_____

_____

_____

_____

Think about a time in the last few months when you did pay attention to pacing yourself and had a better outcome. Describe what happened:

_____

_____

_____

_____

Think about a project you've been avoiding because it seems too overwhelming. Describe how you might tackle that project by breaking it down into smaller pieces and pacing yourself:

_____

_____

_____

_____

_____

One of the factors that influence the pain gate is mood. When you're feeling unhappy, pain tends to bother you more than it would otherwise. Conversely, when you're feeling happier than usual, pain tends to bother you less.

Unfortunately, pain makes it easy to slip into depression; it takes knowledge and skill on your part to avoid this trap or to pull yourself out of it.

When people develop chronic pain, they often quit doing some of the activities that contributed to their happiness and well-being. For example, they may cut back on work, hobbies, and sports.

They also may withdraw from social activities or push others away with the irritable mood that tends to accompany pain. Often, self-esteem decreases with the perception of being less productive or less able to do fun activities with friends or family.

Thus, chronic pain can set into motion a vicious cycle of pain leading to depressed mood, leading to a more open pain gate. This then leads to even less productivity, less exercise and recreation, and less enjoyable interaction, causing more depression and more pain, and so on.

To effectively deal with chronic pain, it's therefore necessary to become skilled at mood regulation. Chronic pain doesn't have to lead to depression, but it certainly puts more demand on your mood management skills. For this reason, please review again Chapter 2, Mood Regulation, to refresh your memory of what some of these skills are.

Then turn to the worksheet that follows and write down some plans for using mood regulation strategies to better manage your pain.

Pick at least two of the mood improvement strategies below and write a brief plan for using them over the next few weeks to see if improving your mood helps you deal better with pain.

Increase enjoyable activities and social interactions:

_____

_____

_____

Perform acts of kindness:

_____

_____

_____

Smile and laugh:

_____

_____

_____

Decrease self-critical thinking:

_____

_____

_____

Practice gratitude:

_____

_____

_____

Chronic pain usually leads people to decrease their physical activity level. This can happen for several reasons.

People may have been told to rest after the onset of an injury or illness, but then they kept up this inactive lifestyle way longer than necessary or helpful. Often people decrease activity because specific movements in the past have triggered increases in pain. Sometimes the decreased activity occurs as a result of people giving up their normal roles, such as work or regular participation in sports or other recreational activities. And sometimes inactivity is a result of the depressed mood that often develops as a result of chronic pain.

While it's understandable how a physically inactive lifestyle can develop in persons with chronic pain, it's important to recognize that this inactivity can set off several vicious cycles that only make pain worse. For example, inactivity can result in weakening and shrinking of muscles and tendons in ways that make some pain conditions worse (Figure 7.2).

Inactivity can also deprive people of natural pain-relieving reactions that occur in the body as a result of exercise. For example, the good feeling that most people experience during and after exercise comes at least partly from the release of *endorphins*, which are the body's own natural pain-relieving chemicals. As the inactive body produces less of these endorphins, pain increases, which leads to even less activity. Inactivity leaves more time for the brain to focus on pain, which adds to pain suffering, leading to even less activity.

Figure 7.2

Pain–inactivity–weakness cycle.

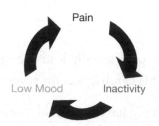

Figure 7.3

Pain–inactivity–low mood cycle.

Movement and exercise are also important to mood. Inactivity often leads to worsening of mood, which tends to open the pain gate and increase pain suffering. The more these negative effects of inactivity increase pain, the less active chronic pain sufferers tend to be, which leads to even more pain (Figure 7.3).

The way out of these vicious cycles is to find, with the guidance of your healthcare providers, safe activities you can do to increase strength and flexibility, release endorphins, increase your energy level, give your brain something to focus on besides pain, and improve your mood.

In consulting with your healthcare providers, make sure you openly discuss fears you have about worsening your pain condition through movement and exercise. Such fear is so common that it's been given its own name: *kinesiophobia*. Often such fears are no longer warranted, but you may need some specific reassurance in order to commit to becoming more active.

If you still have doubts about the value of movement and exercise for chronic pain, search the Internet for "exercise and pain relief," looking especially at more reputable sites such as http://www.webmd.com. You might also look up the pioneering pain psychology work of Dr. Wilbert Fordyce, who showed the importance of gradually increasing exercise intensity and duration according to a plan worked out with healthcare professionals, rather than allowing pain to dictate the amount you exercise.

In developing a plan for increasing movement and exercise, it's important to pay attention to the concept of activity pacing discussed earlier in this chapter. So please review this again to make sure you don't set yourself up for failure by overdoing when you're just starting.

Also, you may want to review Chapter 1, Self-Management: Changing Behavior and Thoughts, for strategies to motivate yourself to follow through on your plans for increasing movement and exercise.

Now complete the following worksheet to help you understand, and more effectively use, the pain management strategy of movement.

Describe in your own words (or in words and a drawing) one of the vicious cycles that can occur as a result of not being physically active enough:

_____

_____

_____

_____

_____

Describe in your own words (or in words and a drawing) another of the vicious cycles that can occur as a result of not being physically active enough:

_____

_____

_____

_____

Describe a plan for gradually increasing your movement and exercise over the next few weeks and state how you'll check this plan out with your healthcare providers:

_____

_____

_____

_____

_____

_____

_____

_____

Tension and stress contribute to another pain-related vicious cycle (Figure 7.4). Pain is stressful and leads to tension, but stress and tension push the pain gate more open and increase pain suffering, which leads to more stress and tension. The way out of this vicious cycle involves learning and applying skills for managing stress and reducing tension.

Our bodies respond physically to stress, often with muscle tightness. Tense muscles can aggravate some kinds of pain and can use up energy that we might need for other tasks.

To manage pain well, it's important to learn to recognize when you're becoming stressed and to practice stress management techniques. You may want to review again Chapter 3, Stress and Anxiety Management, to help you decide which techniques you'll try as part of your effort to find pain management solutions that work for you. Some of the most effective relaxation techniques are summarized here for your convenience:

- **Relaxing your muscles**: Consciously relax each of your muscle groups (e.g., starting at the head and working down the body). Pay special attention to common tension locations such as the forehead, jaw muscles, hands, and shoulders. Smooth your forehead, unclench your jaw and fists, put a slight smile on the corners of your mouth, and let your shoulders relax and drop into a more comfortable position.

- **Relaxing your breathing**: Breathe slowly and deeply, remembering to push your stomach outward as you inhale.

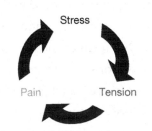

Figure 7.4

Stress–tension–pain cycle.

This allows you to inflate your lungs more fully, so you can breathe more slowly. Instead of breathing about 14 times a minute like most people, or about 18 times a minute like a stressed person, work toward a slower, more relaxed breathing rhythm of 6 to 10 times per minute. If you can, try to spend a little longer blowing the air out, as this is the most relaxing part of the breath cycle. Breathing in this way will turn down your body's fight-or-flight response system and allow you to relax more fully and let go of some tension. Smartphone users can find helpful training apps for relaxed breathing, such as Breathe2Relax. If you have medical problems that affect your ability to breathe deeply, talk with your healthcare providers about the use of this method of relaxation.

Relaxing with mental imagery: Stress can also be calmed by imagining yourself in a peaceful, beautiful place or by picturing someone whose image brings up feelings of calmness and happiness. If you visualize a place, it can be one that you've actually been to, one you've seen in a picture or movie, or one you invent by just using your imagination. Some people imagine taking a walk along a beautiful, tree-lined path. Others imagine visiting the beach or a peaceful river or lake. Make this experience as real as possible by imagining as many details as you can. For example, imagine the look of the sky, the beautiful colors you see, the enjoyable scents you notice, and the pleasant temperature of the air around you. Relax in this place for a while and enjoy your visit. When you're ready to leave your imaginary place, readjust by slowly opening your eyes and gently moving your body, noticing the things around you as you end your relaxing imaginary journey.

Relaxing with meditation: Meditation is another mental stress-reduction technique that can help to narrow the pain gate. One form of meditation involves silent mental repetition of a word or short phrase, often called a "mantra." Sometimes Sanskrit words, such as *om*, are used, but English words, such as *relax* or *calm*, work as well. This practice can be combined with the muscle relaxation and breathing exercises just described. With your eyes closed and muscles relaxed, spend a few minutes silently repeating "relax" or another mantra each time you exhale. It's normal for your mind to wander to other topics as you meditate. When you notice this happening, gently bring your attention back to your breath and mantra. With practice, your brain will grow more skilled at remaining focused during meditation.

- **Practicing mindfulness**: As you may recall from Chapter 3, Stress and Anxiety Management, *mindfulness* is both a type of meditation and an approach to life in general that involves awareness and appreciation of the present moment, rather than unproductive focus on the past or future. Mindfulness training encourages a relaxed attitude of acceptance and nonjudgmental observation as an alternative to emotional overreactivity. A mindful approach to pain involves observing any pain-related emotions, bodily sensations, thoughts, and images as they come up and allowing them to pass through awareness without acting reflexively on them. A mindful perspective makes it easier to endure the temporary discomfort of pain, knowing that these pain-related emotions, sensations, thoughts, and images will pass. Mindfulness training programs, such as Mindfulness Based Stress Reduction (MBSR), have been shown in research studies to have beneficial effects for persons with chronic pain. Brain imaging research has even demonstrated that meditation causes growth in the brain regions responsible for dampening pain. Apps and additional training on meditation and mindfulness are available on the Internet (e.g., https://www.headspace.com and https://insighttimer.com), and training programs are available in many communities.

Now complete the following worksheet to help you plan ways to effectively use the pain self-management strategy of relaxation.

■ **Relaxation Planning Worksheet**

Pick at least two of the relaxation strategies below that seem interesting to you, and write a brief plan for using them over the next few weeks to see if relaxation helps you deal better with pain.

Relaxing your muscles:

_____

_____

_____

Relaxing your breathing:

_____

_____

_____

Relaxing with mental imagery:

_____

_____

_____

Relaxing with meditation:

_____

_____

_____

Practicing mindfulness:

_____

_____

_____

Pain makes it harder to sleep; more than half of chronic pain sufferers report difficulty falling asleep, staying asleep, or both. The reasons for this are multiple:

- Pain can make it more difficult to find a comfortable position for falling asleep.

- Pain can also develop or worsen during the course of sleep from staying in certain positions for too long or from moving in ways that aggravate the pain.

- Because of worry about medical, financial, or other issues related to pain, it may be difficult to relax enough to fall asleep.

- The depressed mood that often occurs in people with chronic pain can interfere with sleep, commonly causing early-morning awakening.

- Being upset about inability to sleep can make falling asleep even more difficult.

Often, the ineffective pain coping strategies that people use can unintentionally result in more difficulty sleeping:

- One of these ineffective pain coping strategies is napping excessively during the day. People with chronic pain often nap out of boredom or an attempt to escape from pain or unhappiness. They may nap because drowsiness is a side effect of many pain medications or because they're trying to make up for poor sleep the night before. Unfortunately, napping too much disrupts the brain's built-in "clock," making it harder to fall asleep at night.

- Another ineffective pain coping strategy is staying indoors too much and not getting enough exposure to bright morning light. Excessive time indoors disrupts the brain's built-in clock, which relies on natural cycles of light and dark to stay calibrated.

- Many people with chronic pain spend too much time in bed during the day, passing time by watching TV, reading, or using tablets, smartphones, or laptops. This excessive time in bed while awake weakens the association the brain makes between bed and sleep, so the head hitting the pillow at night no longer serves as a trigger to fall asleep.

■ And some people with chronic pain drink alcohol at night, hoping this will allow them to fall asleep despite their pain. The trouble with this pain coping strategy is that alcohol consumed to help fall asleep often makes it more difficult to sleep soundly throughout the night.

Unfortunately, lack of restful sleep makes it harder to cope with pain, setting up another vicious cycle in which pain leads to difficulty sleeping, which leads to greater pain suffering and even more difficulty sleeping. The way out of this vicious cycle is to learn and apply skills for improving sleep, while also using the other pain self-management strategies described in this chapter.

As you sleep better, you'll cope better with the pain you still have, and as you manage pain better, you'll sleep better. Research-proven strategies for improving sleep are explained next.

Create a Proper Sleeping Environment

Most people sleep better in a cool and dark bedroom. A fan or air conditioner may help during hot times of the year, and the thermostat should be set to a cool temperature at night during cold times of the year.

Unless there's a safety reason requiring a nightlight, it's best to keep the bedroom dark, even to the point of covering or turning away illuminated displays on clocks. If there are lights outside of the bedroom windows, close the blinds or curtains and, if necessary, use room-darkening curtain liners.

Most people also sleep better in a quiet bedroom. If a bed partner snores, or if other noises are present, earplugs may be necessary for restful sleep. If a bed partner snores loudly, makes gasping sounds, and still seems tired in the morning, this might indicate a serious but correctible problem. Encourage him or her to ask a healthcare provider whether an evaluation for obstructive sleep apnea is warranted.

Incidentally, if you've been told you have this same type of snoring problem, you should also ask about being evaluated. Uncorrected obstructive sleep apnea can leave you feeling more fatigued and make it harder to cope with chronic pain, in addition to causing other serious health problems.

If you have trouble falling asleep due to physical discomfort, ask your healthcare providers about ideas for the best sleeping positions and use of support pillows or a better mattress for your condition.

Many people with chronic pain develop habits that interfere with sleep. For example, they may watch TV in bed either to help them fall asleep or to pass time when they lie awake in pain. Or they may spend time during the day resting in bed to relieve pain. Unfortunately, the more activities of this type that occur in bed or in the bedroom, the less likely the brain will form a strong association between the bedroom and sleep. It generally works best to watch TV, read, and use smartphones and other electronic devices in another room so that the brain more strongly links being in bed with sleep.

Be Smart about Foods, Beverages, and Medicines

If you have trouble sleeping, avoid stimulants, such as caffeine, in the afternoon and evening. Caffeinated drinks include coffee, tea, colas and some other soft drinks, energy drinks, and some weight-loss products.

Many people with chronic pain develop the habit of consuming alcohol before going to bed, with the belief that this will help them sleep. While it's true that for many people alcohol does help with falling asleep, it also reduces the quality of sleep, causing people to get less deep and restful sleep.

Alcohol also commonly causes people to have difficulty remaining asleep through the night. Therefore, alcohol should not be consumed within 3 hours of going to bed and should be consumed in moderation, if at all, before then.

No heavy meals or snacks should be consumed within 2 to 3 hours before bedtime because digestion interferes with sleep. If hungry before bed, try a light snack of carbohydrates, perhaps with a little protein.

The old-time remedy of a glass of warm milk before bed doesn't appear to have any special chemical magic, but warm milk still may help those who find it psychologically relaxing.

Talk to your healthcare providers about a safe plan to decrease nighttime urination. This might involve changing medications or the time of administration of some medications, as well as decreased fluid consumption before sleep. This can help to reduce the problem of difficulty falling back asleep after you've gotten up to use the bathroom.

Talk to your healthcare providers and do your own research regarding any prescription or over-the-counter sleep medications you take, as many of these are only designed to be used for short periods of time and have potentially serious side effects.

Antidepressant medications may help with sleep in persons for whom sleep disturbance is a symptom of depression. Certain antidepressant medications have sedating side effects and may also help with sleep even for those who are not clinically depressed. If interested, talk to your healthcare providers about whether these might be helpful for you.

Relax and Unwind before Bed

Exercise is generally helpful for sleep, especially exercise early in the day with exposure to bright daylight. It's not wise, however, to do strenuous exercise within 3 to 4 hours of going to bed, as this tends to make it more difficult to fall asleep.

Sleep researchers have discovered that exposure to light from certain electronic devices, such as TVs, computer screens, and smartphones, can make it harder for the brain to fall asleep. Therefore, it's best to discontinue these activities an hour or two before going to bed and instead do calming activities, such as reading or listening to relaxing music.

If you have the time, a warm bath can also help your body and mind feel ready to drift off to sleep.

Relax While in Bed

Once you're in bed, it helps to practice some of the relaxation skills described earlier in Chapter 3, Stress and Anxiety Management. For example, relaxing your muscles or visualizing soothing imagery can help you drift off to sleep. Slow, rhythmic breathing from the diaphragm also helps. You'll know if you're doing this correctly if your stomach rises each time you inhale and falls back down when you exhale. Meditation can be combined with muscle relaxation and breathing, perhaps by mentally repeating the word *relax* each time you exhale.

As you're relaxing, allow sleep to come naturally. It's best not to try too hard to fall asleep, as this effort actually makes falling asleep more difficult. You may remind yourself that, even if you don't fall asleep, you're still gaining valuable rest through your practice of relaxation and meditation.

If worrisome thoughts come to you as you're falling asleep or sometime during the night, you might try jotting them down on a notepad by your bed. This sometimes allows the mind to temporarily let the worries go, knowing they'll be dealt with the next day.

Limit Your Time in Bed

Many people with chronic pain spend excessive amounts of time in bed. Because they have trouble falling asleep or remaining asleep, they sleep well past their normal awakening time or take long naps during the day.

While it's understandable that people would do this to try to catch up on missed sleep, research has shown that this is actually not a wise strategy. Even though it seems counterintuitive, restricting time in bed eventually results in better sleep quality.

Guidelines to follow are listed below:

- Go to bed only when you feel sleepy.

- If you don't fall asleep within about 20 minutes, leave the bedroom and do something relaxing, such as reading, until you feel sleepy again. Watching TV or playing video games is generally not a good idea because it's likely to be too stimulating and because light from the TV or computer screen can interfere with sleep. The reason to get up and leave the bedroom is that your brain won't learn to associate the bed with frustration over inability to sleep. Return to bed only when you feel drowsy.

- Limit your total time in bed to 7 hours or less while you're trying to re-establish a healthy sleep–wake cycle. Once you're sleeping better, you can increase your sleep time to around 8 hours. Research generally supports 7 to 8 hours as the optimal amount of sleep for most adults, while adolescents and young adults seem to function best with about 9 hours of sleep. Talk to your healthcare providers about this in case your particular health condition requires a different amount of sleep.

- Make sure you get up at approximately the same time every day, including on weekends, whether you slept well or not. This helps to keep your internal clock regulated.

- Try to minimize naps during the day. Especially avoid any naps longer than 20 to 30 minutes, as long naps disrupt the sleep–wake cycle. Afternoon naps are generally better for you than morning or evening naps.

Use the following worksheet to plan how you'll implement some of these sleep improvement strategies.

For at least two of the categories below, list one or more specific sleep improvement methods you think might help you. Write a specific plan for trying out each method over the next few weeks.

Create a proper sleeping environment:

_____

_____

_____

Be smart about foods, beverages, and medicines:

_____

_____

_____

Relax and unwind before bed:

_____

_____

_____

Relax while in bed:

_____

_____

_____

Limit your time in bed:

_____

_____

_____

Pain research demonstrates what many pain sufferers have already noticed: Pain is experienced more intensely when we focus on it and recedes more into the background when we focus on something else.

For example, one interesting study showed that both pain level and activation of the brain's pain centers were reduced while subjects played a virtual reality video game.

This is why healthcare professionals often try to distract patients while performing painful procedures. This is also why persons with chronic pain often notice that they weren't as aware of their pain when they were deeply engaged in a stimulating conversation, an engrossing movie or video game, or an enjoyable physical activity.

In chronic pain sufferers, a vicious cycle often develops in which pain leads to giving up many activities and interests, which leaves little else to focus on but pain (Figure 7.5). This leads to greater experience of pain suffering, even more withdrawal from activities and interests, and so on.

The solution to this vicious cycle is to creatively and systematically plan and implement a richer daily schedule of activities that will not cause physical harm but will keep your mind engaged and engrossed.

Use the worksheet that follows to help you understand why shifting your focus away from pain works, to become aware of how much time you focus on things besides pain already, and to plan more activities that might engage your attention over the next few weeks.

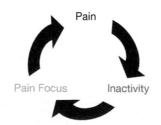

Figure 7.5

Pain–inactivity–pain focus cycle.

■ **Focus Shifting Worksheet**

Describe in your own words (or in words and a drawing) the vicious cycle that can happen when people focus on their pain:

_____

_____

_____

_____

_____

_____

Without trying to change what you normally do, estimate how much time you spend focusing on things other than pain over the next two days:

■ Day 1: Percentage of the day in which your main focus was on something other than pain: _____%

■ Day 2: Percentage of the day in which your main focus was something other than pain: _____%

List some things you can focus on to take your attention off pain even more often. Write some specific plans for trying this out over the next few days:

_____

_____

_____

_____

_____

_____

_____

_____

_____

_____

_____

Pain behaviors are what people do to show others that they're in pain. Examples include:

- Pained facial expressions, such as frowns and furrowed brows

- Sighs, grunts, and moans

- Grabbing or massaging of body parts

- Tense muscles

- Slow or stiff movements

- Slumped body posture

- Comments about pain

These pain behaviors are learned in childhood as a useful way to communicate distress and to elicit help for acute injury or illness. When pain is chronic, however, pain behaviors often serve little purpose and can, in fact, be counterproductive.

One way pain behaviors can be counterproductive is that people tend to feel the way they act. When people with chronic pain frown, tense up, slump over, or otherwise act like they're suffering greatly, they tend to suffer more.

By contrast, when they smile, relax, and adopt an upright posture, they tend to feel happier and more energetic.

For an entertaining and informative presentation on this topic, search with your Internet browser for a TED Talk by social psychologist Dr. Amy Cuddy, entitled "Your Body Language Shapes Who You Are."

Another reason to minimize pain behavior is that others will generally react to you in a more positive way if you come across as cheerful and energetic than if you come across as miserable and exhausted. This then leads to better-quality relationships that engage your attention and take your focus off of pain.

You can still communicate honestly with healthcare providers and those closest to you to let them know how you're doing, but you'll generally be better off if you minimize pain behaviors in most of your interactions.

Many people aren't fully aware of their own pain behaviors, so it's helpful to ask others what they observe.

Use the following worksheet to become more aware of the pain behaviors you're exhibiting on a regular basis and to formulate a plan for reducing these pain behaviors.

▢ Pain Behavior Reduction Worksheet

List the pain behaviors you're aware of exhibiting:

_____

_____

List the pain behaviors that others who know you well tell you they've observed:

_____

_____

List one pain behavior you want to work on reducing first:

_____

_____

Over the next day, keep a rough count of the number of times you exhibit that particular pain behavior. Don't try to change how often you do it. Just count and then come back and report here how many times you did it:

_____

_____

List a more adaptive behavior you'll display in place of the maladaptive pain behavior (e.g., smiling instead of frowning):

_____

_____

Now try reducing the frequency of the pain behavior you've identified and report the approximate number of times you exhibit that pain behavior on the next three days:

Day 1: _____

Day 2: _____

Day 3: _____

Physical pain management strategies include use of proper body mechanics and ergonomics, as well as various body self-care activities, such as stretching, icing, and drinking enough fluids.

Body mechanics refers to the way you use your body to lift, push, pull, and perform other movements to get things done. Common body mechanics recommendations include using your legs instead of your back when lifting objects, keeping heavy objects close to you when lifting or carrying, and not twisting your spine when lifting.

Ergonomics refers to the design, arrangement, and proper use of furniture, equipment, and tools to get things done more safely, comfortably, and efficiently. An ergonomics evaluator might encourage you to keep your computer monitor at a proper height to reduce neck strain or to use a chair that provides lumbar support to reduce back and neck pain.

Instruction and training in the use of proper body mechanics and ergonomics is provided by physical therapists, occupational therapists, and others with specialized training in this field. These experts can give you specific guidance on ways to minimize your particular pain condition, as well as to avoid new injuries, through use of proper body mechanics and ergonomics.

Physical therapists, occupational therapists, physicians, and other healthcare providers can also give you guidance on use of other physical pain management methods, such as application of heat or cold, stretches, physical exercise, and self-massage.

Healthcare professionals can also provide helpful direction regarding the substances you put into your body. For many pain conditions, for example, it's important to drink enough fluids to keep the body properly hydrated.

Weight control can make a big difference for many people with lower back pain or pain in the knees or other joints of the lower body.

Smoking cessation is also important. Smokers are more likely to experience chronic pain. Their pain tends to be more intense than that of nonsmokers and to interfere more with social and work functioning. Tobacco use is known to delay healing and to accelerate degeneration of body parts, such as the discs in the spine, involved in common types of pain.

These physical interventions are included in this chapter because they fall under the category of pain self-management skills and techniques. Like the other topics included in this chapter, these are skills and techniques that you can learn and apply on a daily basis to help manage chronic pain.

All too often, persons with chronic pain don't consistently use these types of self-management skills and techniques. Because they're not complete cures for the pain and only provide temporary relief, the skills and techniques are often overlooked or forgotten.

If you have a pain condition that can't be cured but must be lived with, then it's important to regularly use several of the self-management strategies covered in this chapter. Even if a particular strategy only helps by a few percentage points, if you combine multiple strategies, they add up to major relief and improvement in well-being and productivity.

And just because they need to be done on an ongoing basis, remember that this is no different from other basic life functions, such as eating and breathing.

Complete the following worksheet to think more about physical pain self-management strategies and develop plans for using them more regularly.

You may want to quickly review Chapter 1, Self-Management: Changing Behavior and Thoughts, to brush up on ways to motivate yourself to follow through on your plans for more regular use of these physical pain self-management strategies.

■ Physical Pain Management Strategies Worksheet

Think about some of the activities that tend to cause your pain to flare up and write them down here:

_____

_____

_____

Talk to your healthcare providers or do other research to try to come up with plans for doing some of these activities with greater attention to body mechanics and ergonomics. Write your plan here:

_____

_____

_____

_____

Think of some physical methods for providing temporary pain relief that you can do on your own and that your healthcare providers have advised you to do. Examples include use of heat or cold, stretches, physical exercise, and self-massage. List the methods here in order of how helpful they have been or how helpful you think they might be:

_____

_____

_____

_____

Describe your plans for using one or more of these physical pain management methods more often over the next few weeks:

_____

_____

_____

_____

Pain medications are a double-edged sword. All of them have some potential to help with management of pain, but all can cause problematic side effects. Your job is to work with your prescribing healthcare providers to find the right balance between helpful effects and undesirable side effects or other long-term problems.

Many pain medications are derived from the same poppy plant used to make opium and heroin. These narcotic medications are sometimes called "opiates" or "opioids." Examples include morphine, hydrocodone, oxycodone, and codeine, but you may also know them by their various brand names.

These medications are now generally considered most helpful for short-term pain, such as pain following surgery. Their value for long-term, or chronic, pain is a matter of some debate, but they are still widely prescribed for chronic pain.

These narcotic medications can help to reduce the pain that medication users feel and also reduce how much they care about the pain they still have. But some users find that these medications also leave them caring less about other things in life, and the resulting apathy and low motivation can reduce productivity and social engagement.

These narcotic medications tend to cause side effects such as constipation and can impair mental alertness, making it less safe for users to do activities such as driving.

And they can, over time, become less effective, requiring higher and higher doses for the same pain relief. Addiction can be a problem for some users, and each year thousands of people die from overdosing on prescription narcotics.

Non-narcotic prescription pain medications, such as gabapentin, are being used more frequently, especially to target nerve pain. Medications in this class can still cause side effects such as drowsiness and mental dullness, so their pain-relieving benefit needs to be balanced out with any loss of mental acuity.

Even over-the-counter pain medications, such as anti-inflammatories (ibuprofen, naproxen, etc.) and acetaminophen, can, over time and in higher doses, cause harm to vital organs, such as the liver and the kidneys.

To manage pain wisely, therefore, it's important to honestly examine what your medications' beneficial effects are and what their harmful effects are. You can talk to your pharmacist or do your own research on reputable websites such as https://www.drugs.com to find out more information about side effects.

In consultation with your healthcare providers, figure out whether you're better off with, or without, pain medications, and determine what dosages work best to maximize relief while minimizing harmful side effects.

Sometimes it's difficult to know whether medications are still helpful when you've been on them for a long time, so you and your prescriber might discuss trying to taper off a medication to see if you really need it. Usually such experiments are best done one medication at a time.

Don't stop taking medications without consulting your prescribing healthcare providers, since going "cold turkey" can sometimes cause very unpleasant, or even dangerous, drug withdrawal effects.

Use the following worksheet to think through the pros and cons of your current pain medications and develop a list of questions to ask your prescriber.

For each of your pain medications, list the ways it helps you feel better or function better. Pay special attention to whether or not the medication actually helps you function better, such as being more productive and having better-quality interactions with family and friends. Some medications may dull your pain but leave you less able to function.

What problems does the medication seem to cause you? Talk to your pharmacist or do your own research about that medication's harmful side effects or other problems of long-term use.

Then develop a list of questions or concerns to discuss with your prescriber to make sure you want to stay on that particular medication at that dosage.

Medication 1: _____

    Helpful effects:

_____

_____

_____

    Harmful effects:

_____

_____

_____

    Questions or concerns to discuss with your prescriber:

_____

_____

_____

Medication 2: _____

    Helpful effects:

_____

_____

_____

Harmful effects:

_____

_____

_____

_____

Questions or concerns to discuss with your prescriber:

_____

_____

_____

_____

Medication 3: _____

Helpful effects:

_____

_____

_____

_____

Harmful effects:

_____

_____

_____

_____

Questions or concerns to discuss with your prescriber:

_____

_____

_____

_____

Some people are not comfortable directly expressing or dealing with their emotions. When these people develop an injury or illness, they sometimes become highly focused on physical symptoms as a way to communicate unhappiness or other emotions to others. Instead of admitting to being depressed, for example, they might talk at length about their aches and pains.

Or they may become very focused on physical symptoms, including pain, as a way to avoid facing the uncomfortable emotions in themselves.

Or, if they are not comfortable assertively expressing what they like and don't like, they may use pain as an indirect way to communicate this. For example, they may use pain expression to receive more of what they want, such as attention or support. Or they may use pain expression to avoid what they don't want, such as unpleasant chores, uncomfortable social interactions, or pressure to achieve.

If pain serves a purpose for you like any of those just described, you may end up more focused on your pain than you need to be. One way to decrease your attention to pain is to make sure it's not serving one of these purposes.

So if you think you're not comfortable expressing your emotions, try writing for a few minutes a day about how you feel (your emotions, that is, not your pain or other physical symptoms). Extensive research has documented the health benefits of writing about deeply felt emotions; much of this research is by psychologist Dr. James Pennebaker, who has written a useful book on this topic: *Opening Up by Writing It Down*. After you've gotten more comfortable with expressing your feelings by writing about them, find someone you feel safe with to practice talking about these feelings.

If you think it's possible that you're focusing on physical symptoms as a way to avoid uncomfortable emotions, try to deliberately interrupt your focus on physical symptoms and think about what emotions might be just under the surface. Emotions that are often avoided include sadness, worry, hurt, anger, and guilt. Becoming more aware of and directly expressing such emotions may help you let go of some of your focus on pain or other physical symptoms. If you want more information about this approach to pain management, there are several interesting books available on this topic written by Dr. John Sarno.

If pain symptoms are serving as an indirect way of asking for what you want or don't want, begin practicing assertively saying to others what these preferences are. When being assertive, it helps to communicate using "*I* statements," such as "I like it when you _____" or "I'd prefer not to _____."

When you communicate this way, others are less likely to react defensively. You might want to go back to Chapter 4, Anger and Frustration Management, and review the section "Assertive Communication."

Use the following worksheet to increase your understanding of how well you recognize and express emotions instead of using physical symptoms to avoid dealing with them.

Expression of Emotions Worksheet

Over the next two days, try to keep track of how much you are aware of physical symptoms such as pain compared to your awareness of emotions such as sadness, worry, hurt, anger, and guilt. Write your estimate below.

- Time spent being aware of physical symptoms: _____

- Time spent being aware of emotions: _____

Over the next two days, try to keep track of how much you talk about physical symptoms such as pain and how much you talk about emotions such as sadness, worry, hurt, anger, and guilt. Write your estimate below.

- Time spent talking about physical symptoms: _____

- Time spent talking about emotions: _____

Over the next two days, try to keep track of how many times expression of physical symptoms such as pain allows you to get something you want or avoid something you don't want. Write your estimate below.

- Times your expression of pain or other physical symptoms allowed you to get something you wanted: _____

- Times your expression of pain or other physical symptoms allowed you to avoid something you didn't want: _____

Pick one of these incidents and write something you could have said to communicate your preference instead of using your physical symptoms:

_____

_____

_____

_____

_____

_____

_____

_____

Chronic pain often leads sufferers to restrict social and recreational involvement. Over time, this restricted activity and reduced involvement in enjoyable activities can end up making the pain suffering worse. This happens because the brain focuses more on pain when it doesn't have something better to focus on. It also happens because lack of sufficient enjoyable activity contributes to depressed mood, which further opens the pain gate.

As you can see, this contributes to another vicious cycle. Pain leads to withdrawal from activities, which leads to more focus on pain and more depressed mood, which leads to more pain suffering, and so on.

The longer formerly enjoyed activities are avoided, the harder they are to resume because of loss of momentum, loss of confidence, and weakened social connections with former activity partners.

The solution is to break this vicious cycle as soon as you recognize it by gradually resuming some of the activities and social involvement you previously enjoyed, as well as trying some new ones. At first you may feel less enjoyment than before, but with time, the pleasure will begin to return, your mood will improve, and your brain will focus less on pain. Chapter 2, Mood Regulation, should be reviewed for more discussion about resuming former activities and trying out new ones.

Keep in mind that even brief social encounters, such as saying "hello" to someone in the elevator or smiling as you pass a stranger, can be helpful.

On the following worksheet, list some activities and social ties from which you've withdrawn. Then list some of the activities you're willing to resume and what modifications in these activities you might have to make. Also list some new recreational and social activities you might learn to enjoy. And finally, list some specific plans for starting to pull yourself out of this vicious cycle.

■ Socialization and Recreation Worksheet

List some social and recreational activities you've withdrawn from since you developed chronic pain:

_____

_____

_____

_____

_____

List the activities you're willing to resume, even if you have to modify how you do them. Also list any modifications you plan to make:

_____

_____

_____

_____

_____

List some new social and recreational activities you're willing to try:

_____

_____

_____

_____

_____

List the specific steps you plan to take this week to increase your social and recreational involvement:

_____

_____

_____

_____

_____

The same pain signal can be perceived differently depending on what and how you're thinking. Certain types of pain beliefs and attitudes promote adjustment to pain, while others get in the way of adjustment.

Take a few minutes to complete the questionnaire in Table 7.1 about your pain beliefs and attitudes.

Table 7.1 Pain Beliefs Inventory

Please indicate how much you **agree** or **disagree** with the following statements:

1. Totally <u>agree</u>   2. Mostly agree   3. Agree somewhat   4. Mostly disagree   5. Totally <u>disagree</u>

1. _____ My pain makes it impossible to do anything constructive.

2. _____ My pain makes it impossible to be happy.

3. _____ My pain could be completely cured if only I could find the right doctor or the right treatment.

4. _____ I am probably wasting my time in seeking help for my pain.

5. _____ It is primarily the responsibility of the medical profession to relieve my pain.

6. _____ There is very little I can do to ease my pain.

7. _____ My pain could be a sign of a serious medical problem that my doctors have not properly diagnosed.

8. _____ If only I could get rid of my pain, life would be wonderful.

9. _____ It is unfair that I have been singled out to suffer so much pain.

10. _____ In some ways I may deserve to suffer from pain because of wrong things I have done in my life.

11. _____ It is best to avoid all painful activity so I do not cause more injury.

12. _____ My family and friends should offer me support and comfort when I am in pain.

13. _____ My attitudes and emotions influence how much I suffer from my pain.

14. _____ People suffer more from pain when there is little else in their lives to focus on.

Now go back and look to see if you endorsed any of the first twelve items with a score of 1 or 2, or one or both of the last two items with a score of 4 or 5. If so, please read the following worksheet for explanations of why and how these particular pain beliefs could be unhelpful for you. Then write out and practice some more adaptive ways of thinking about your pain.

1. If you believe that your pain makes it impossible to do anything constructive, you're more likely to adopt the role of an invalid who focuses too much on limitations and disability. People generally cope better with chronic pain when they focus on what they're still able to do, rather than focusing on their loss of ability.

   If you endorsed or partially endorsed the belief that pain makes it impossible to do anything constructive, spend a few minutes thinking of some more helpful statements you can make to yourself, such as: "I still can accomplish a lot; I just have to be smarter about how I do things now."

   List your new, more adaptive thoughts here:

   _____

   _____

   _____

   _____

   _____

2. If you believe that pain makes it impossible to be happy, you're more likely to focus on the negative aspects of your situation and not take active steps to do things that will improve your life satisfaction. Chronic pain can make it more challenging to be happy, but many people with chronic pain are quite happy once they learn skills for dealing with pain and regulating their mood.

   Try to come up with some statements you can make to yourself to think more adaptively about pain and happiness, such as: "Pain makes happiness a bigger challenge, but there are still many experiences I can enjoy and much I can feel grateful for in my life."

   List your new, more adaptive thoughts here:

   _____

   _____

   _____

   _____

   _____

   _____

3. If you're focused almost entirely on finding a medical or surgical cure for your pain, you may not be very motivated to learn and use pain self-management strategies. On the other hand, if you recognize that your healthcare providers are limited in what they can do, you're more likely to assume responsibility for actively coping with your pain through use of the skills described in this chapter.

    Think of some statements you can make to counter the belief that you can just wait for a medical or surgical cure for your pain. The new statements you create should encourage thinking about how you can actively help yourself. For example: "My treatment providers have done what they can at this point. I'll still stay alert to new treatment options, but for now, it's mostly up to me to take steps to live a good life despite pain."

    List your new, more adaptive thoughts here:

    _____

    _____

    _____

    _____

    _____

4. Because there's often no one-time fix for chronic pain, it's easy to adopt a hopeless and helpless attitude. If you think your pain situation is hopeless and believe you're helpless to change it, you probably won't put much energy into trying to cope better with it. This belief also may increase anxiety, which in turn can open the pain gate and intensify pain suffering.

    Think of some more helpful ways to talk to yourself about pain coping and write them below. For example: "There may not be a single total cure for my pain, but there are several ways I can manage it better."

    List your new, more adaptive thoughts here:

    _____

    _____

    _____

    _____

    _____

    _____

5. If you believe it's the responsibility of the medical profession to relieve your pain, you're less likely to take an active self-management approach to dealing with it. Even if you don't expect the medical profession to completely cure you, it can be unhelpful to lean on them exclusively for pain relief when there are active pain coping strategies you could be using.

Think of some more adaptive ways you could be talking to yourself about taking responsibility for dealing with your pain, and write them below. For example: "Healthcare providers can sometimes be helpful for my pain, but it's mostly up to me to take active steps every day to cope effectively with it."

List your new, more adaptive thoughts here:

_____

_____

_____

_____

_____

6. The belief that there's little you can do to ease your pain and suffering also limits the effort you put into active pain self-management. There may not be dramatic improvement from any one pain self-management strategy, but several strategies used on a regular basis can add up to a lot of relief.

Think about ways to remind yourself of this and write them below. For example: "I'm not powerless. At any given time, there are several things I can do to decrease my suffering and improve my quality of life."

List your new, more adaptive thoughts here:

_____

_____

_____

_____

_____

7. Some people worry excessively about what's causing their pain (e.g., "What if it's a tumor?"). Such worry opens the pain gate wider, increasing pain suffering and leading to even more worry about health. After getting appropriate reassurance from healthcare providers about what's causing the pain, it's more adaptive to let go of unrealistic worry.

Think of some ways you can talk to yourself about this. For example: "I've been thoroughly checked and given a reasonable explanation for my pain. It's not realistic to keep worrying about cancer."

List your new, more adaptive thoughts here:

_____

_____

_____

_____

_____

_____

8. If you believe pain is the cause of all your problems in life, you may not take steps to correct other sources of unhappiness. Some people seem to focus on pain as a way to avoid facing other uncomfortable issues or feelings. In the long run, though, it's often more productive to quit using pain as a distraction or excuse, face up to the issue that's being avoided, and move on in life.

If you believe preoccupation with pain might be serving an avoidance function for you, think of some more productive ways to talk to yourself about this and write them here. For example: "Pain is just one of the difficult issues I need to deal with. The other realities I have to face and handle include _____."

List your new, more adaptive thoughts here:

_____

_____

_____

_____

_____

_____

9. If you dwell on the unfairness of your injury or pain, the anger this causes in you may push your pain gate more open and intensify your pain suffering. Blaming specific others for causing your pain, or blaming fate for singling you out to have pain fuels unhealthy emotions that open the pain gate wider.

    Think of alternate ways of talking to yourself about blame and write them below. For example: "It's unfortunate that this accident happened, but it's not healthy for me to hold onto blame or to focus on the unfairness of my situation. It's better for me to just let the past go and focus on living as well as possible now."

    List your new, more adaptive thoughts here:

    _____

    _____

    _____

    _____

    _____

    _____

10. Some people who are prone to guilt may interpret their pain as a punishment they deserve. This belief can then hold them back from active use of pain self-management skills.

    If this type of thinking applies to you, try to come up with some more helpful ways of talking to yourself about the guilt and pain. For example: "Yes, it's true that I've done things I now regret, and I'll try very hard not to do them again. The past is the past, though, and everyone makes mistakes. I forgive myself and don't deserve to keep suffering."

    List your new, more adaptive thoughts here:

    _____

    _____

    _____

    _____

    _____

    _____

11. Fear of aggravating your pain by physical activity may actually be adding to your pain-related disability. Right after an injury or the onset of an illness, it's often helpful to rest for a short time, but for many injuries and illnesses it's important to resume activity fairly soon. Are you as active as your healthcare providers have advised you to be?

    If you think you might be holding yourself back from better recovery through excessive fear of re-injury, think of some alternate ways of talking to yourself about this and write them below. For example: "I've been reassured by my healthcare providers that _____ is good for me, and I'll be better off if I follow their advice to stay active."

    List your new, more adaptive thoughts here:

    _____

    _____

    _____

    _____

    _____

    _____

12. The belief that family members and friends should offer support and comfort when you're in pain can be unhelpful in two ways. First, it appears that excessive support and comfort in response to pain expression can make pain and disability worse. This may seem surprising, but keep in mind that our behaviors are heavily influenced by social rewards; if pain behaviors are rewarded, they're more likely to occur again. Researchers have shown, for example, that self-reported pain and activation of pain centers in the brain increase when persons with chronic pain are near their highly nurturing spouse. In other words, pain suffering appears to increase when in the presence of someone who rewards the expression of pain with comfort and support. For chronic pain, it's actually more helpful to encourage those close to you to not be so eager to offer support and comfort in reaction to pain behavior. Instead, ask them to react more positively when you're being active and looking cheerful.

    A second reason this belief can lead to problems is that, if you expect nurturance in response to pain behavior and then don't get it, you'll likely feel anger, frustration, or emotional hurt. These emotions can then push the pain gate more open and intensify pain suffering. You'll be better off reminding yourself that no one owes you a particular kind of response to your pain.

Think of some more adaptive ways you can talk to yourself about support and comfort from others and write them below. For example: "When I was a child and skinned my knees, support and comfort were nice and good for me. Now that I'm grown and have a chronic pain condition, I'm better off if I don't get rewarded for my pain behaviors."

List your new, more adaptive thoughts here:

_____

_____

_____

_____

_____

_____

13. As the pain gate illustrates, pain suffering does vary in response to emotional state. Understanding this is important, because it provides another path for self-management of pain. For example, if you can decrease your anger and improve your mood, there's a good chance you'll decrease your pain suffering.

Think of some more adaptive ways you can talk to yourself about emotions and pain and write them below. For example: "When I'm experiencing extra pain suffering, it's a good idea to check out my emotional state because it might be adding to my suffering. If it is, I'll use some of my strategies for dealing better with these emotions, and this may reduce my pain suffering."

List your new, more adaptive thoughts here:

_____

_____

_____

_____

_____

_____

14. The pain gate is less open when the mind is engrossed in enjoyable social interaction or hobbies. This is very important to know if you have a chronic pain condition. Many people, however, are not aware of this, sometimes stubbornly insisting, "It's all physical pain; my mental state has nothing to do with it." It's more adaptive to recognize that pain experience is usually a result of what happens in both the body and the brain, as this gives you another important way to self-manage pain.

Think of some more adaptive ways to talk to yourself about pain and distraction and write them below. For example: "My brain only has the capacity to pay attention to so much at a time. If I keep myself engaged in activities I enjoy, my brain's pain centers will be less active, and I'll feel better."

List your new, more adaptive thoughts here:

_____

_____

_____

_____

_____

_____

_____

_____

_____

_____

_____

_____

_____

_____

_____

Your pain management ability will continue to strengthen as you practice the 12 strategies covered in this chapter. Use the chart in Figure 7.6 to record how you're doing now and then come back and update it periodically as your skills improve. Place a checkmark within each pie wedge to indicate how well you're using that particular skill. Put your checkmark in the *inner circle* if you consider yourself a beginner at that skill. Use the *middle circle* to show intermediate skill and the *outer circle* to indicate advanced skill.

You might also want to post this chart as a reminder of the various pain management strategies you've found helpful and plan to use on a regular basis.

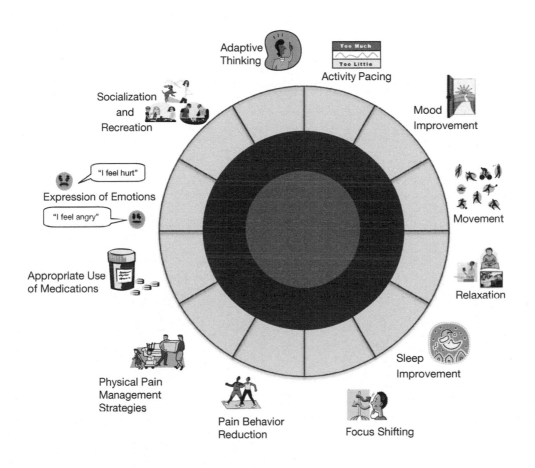

Figure 7.6

Chart for recording twelve pain management strategies.

Epilogue

Congratulations on making your way through to the end of this book. I sincerely hope you've been able to identify and put into practice some new resilience skills that are helping you cope with changes in ability.

We are all works in progress, though, so I encourage you to keep this book handy and refer to it again from time to time as new challenges arise. Review of some of these chapters is also a good idea if you find yourself drifting back to older, less effective coping strategies. As I noted at the beginning, changing habitual ways of thinking and behaving takes hard work. And once you've made these changes, it takes some effort to keep up your positive momentum. Reviewing these chapters periodically can help.

If you ever find yourself getting bogged down, remember, professional help is available (see the section on consulting your healthcare providers in Chapter 2). Often, a little professional guidance and encouragement is all it takes to get yourself back on track.

Index

References to tables and figures are denoted by an italicized *t* and *f*.

CPSIA information can be obtained
at www.ICGtesting.com
Printed in the USA
LVOW04s1412030218
565195LV00005B/28/P